HUGS FROM THE FATHER

Dealing With Loss: The Pathway to Recovery.

BEVERLY CHAHONYO

Copyright © 2021 Beverly Chahonyo

Title: Hugs From The Father
Dealing With Loss: The Pathway to Recovery.

By Beverly Chahonyo

Publisher: Beverly Chahonyo
Photography by: Deji Olatunde of Fotolighouse, Lagos Nigeria
Makeup Artist - Mary of BVASFACES, Lagos Nigeria
Interior Layout Design - House of Kocham
Book Cover Design - Excite Wears

All rights reserved.

No part of this publication may be reproduced or transmitted in any form or by any means, electronic or mechanical, including photocopy, recording or any information storage and retrieval systems, without permission in writing from the publisher.

Scripture taken from The Voice™. Copyright © 2012 by Ecclesia Bible Society. Used by permission. All rights reserved.

ISBN: 978 9966 1745 1 2

Dedication

To my first valentine.
My Daddy.
My heart.
I will forever be a Daddy's Girl.
Thank you for teaching me love.
Thank you for showing me courage.
I will love you forever.

Contents

Acknowledgements

Forward - Bishop Feb Idahosa

Forward - Tabitha Dalizu Chahonyo

Forward - Rachael Bayliss

Forward - Kemi Oye

Introduction

Prologue

Reflections of Seasons Gone: How Bitter Sweet (23)

Reflections of New Beginnings: Finding Beauty in Sadness (29)

Reflections of Finding the Joy in Saying Goodbye (35)

Reflections of Saying Hello: The Other Frank (41)

Reflections of My Tribe (47)

Reflections of Tears that Flow Freely (53)

Reflections of The Queen: Introducing My Amazing Mummy (59)

Reflections of Birthing in the Midst of Mourning (65)

Reflections of My Community (71)

Reflections of Apple Crumble and Coffee (77)

Reflections of How It Really Does Take a Village (83)

(89) Reflections of Amazing Grace and Amazing Love

(95) Reflections of Covering Our Nakedness

(101) Reflections of the Well That Won't Run Dry

(107) Reflections of the Laughter I Never Expected to Hear

(113) Reflections of Birthdays : On Earth and In Heaven

(121) Reflections of Love from Unexpected Places

(127) Reflections of Triggers: Genesis Unknown

(133) Reflections of Angels on Earth

(139) Reflections of Purple Blooms and Celebrating Life

(145) Reflections of The Power To Be

(151) Reflections of Giving Others The Space To Be

(157) Reflections of The Fear of Forgetting

(163) Reflections of Time Stamps

(169) Reflections of Fragrances From My Childhood

(175) Reflections of My Deepest Fear

(181) Reflections of Losing Everything & Gaining Everything

(187) Reflections of Jingle Bells and Christmas Tales

(195) Reflections of Actual Hugs From Actual Fathers

(201) Reflections of New Beginnings With New Friends

(207) Reflections of A Goodbye Kiss: Forever Daddy's Little Girl

(215) Reflections of Me: I am Loved. I am Enough.

Acknowledgements

This book has been in the oven baking for over 3 years. I will try to remember everyone but may not mention you all by name. For those special people who were there in one way or another during those special moments, thank you. I pray that God will do for you exceedingly, abundantly above all you could ask, think or even imagine.

To my Heavenly Father, Creator of heaven and earth, the God of Abraham, Isaac and Jacob. The God of Rachel, Rebecca, Deborah and Ruth; the God of my Mummy and Daddy, and now, God of Bev … to Jesus my Savior and Friend; to the Sweet Holy Spirit, my always companion and advocate … I do not know where I would be if it were not for you. I don't know how I would have survived the season without you. I am beyond grateful for your love, mercy, comfort and strength. I love you.

To my Daddy … my first Valentine, the one who held me up all my life. 3 years and sometimes I still cannot believe it … I will love you fiercely and eternally. Thank you for the gift of you. These words are inspired by you life and a tribute to your legacy through me. They are bitter sweet. With this book our secret place becomes a gift to the world. Thank you. I miss you. I love you.

To my Mummy - my best friend forever. The one who has taught me unconditional love on so many levels. My one-woman cheer squad. The one who rebukes and disciplines me in love. I love you so much. Thank you for showing me how to love and serve God.

To my siblings - what would I be without you? My friends, my protectors, my teachers, my partners in crime. The ones who sharpen me and laugh with me and push me to go harder, higher, faster. I love you all so much!!!!

My munchkins - all seven of you at the time of publication - I am your auntie, your Mummy-Number-Two, your protector, your friend. Thank you for bringing so much joy into our hearts especially during the hardest season of our lives.

To my extended family: my aunties and uncles and cousins - those who came and picked us up and took over and just carried us when we had no strength. To my aunties who wouldn't leave us (especially Mummy) and uncles who helped shield us and guided us to the right decision. Thank you so much. The Lord truly bless you.

To my church and my Mummy's church - words will never be enough. To my Pastor and the entire church family. The Lord repay you according to His measure.

To my tribe - my friends. Those who stepped in during that season and then stepped away. Those who walked the entire journey. Those who sacrificed and travelled and gave of themselves. A million thank yous will never suffice. I leave you to heaven. May you get replenished. To those who still call, those who still remember, those who still let me cry - thank you for your kindness. I love you all.

A special thank you to the angels who saw this as an investment, and sent a financial contribution towards the publication of this book. Almost four years later in the making, and this dream would not have come true without you.

To my publishers and the team around me including those who helped edit and critique and design - you know how much you have pushed me. Thank you. You know how much you mean to me. Thank you.

To my mentor - thank you. I honor you.

To those precious ones who took the time to write a foreword. You have sown deeply and touched my softest spot. Thank you.

Finally, to everyone who will read this book: I pray for your healing be it emotional, spiritual, physical, financial - whatever you lost, I pray that this will truly be the pathway to recover for you.

You are LOVED

You are E. N. O. U. G. H.

Forewords

Not long ago I listened to a beautiful poem by Beverly Chahonyo called The Affair. In that poem, she introduced the listener line by line, to her dance and affair, with grief. Using her intricately crafted words, she described with agonizing accuracy, the pain which so many of us have felt or will one day feel, when we encounter the loss of a loved one. The poem was flawless in its delivery of one major thought—you can make peace with grief and will eventually be strong enough to get past the agony. You can move beyond the hurt presented by grief and not allow it to become your identity because daily, it does get better.

That poem was my first introduction to Hugs from The Father, which is a compilation of the powerful thoughts, arresting ideas, reflections of the journey which Beverly embarked on as she learned to deal with her loss. I found that the words in the book rang true because I remember also walking the same road which she was walking when she penned them.

I have had to deal with loss and grief two times in my life so far; first with the loss of my father when I was 25 years old, and 9 years later when I lost my first son just 12 hours after he was born. It is moments like those which make people ask you if God really is good like you claim He is. They asked me. Some even asked if God was using my loss to teach me a lesson because of a mistake I made.

Here is the good news which I learned through my experience and also from reading God's Word: God does not allow you to experience loss and send grief to you simply because He wants to teach you a lesson, neither does He allow you to experience loss as a punishment for your sins. To describe God in that way would be to reduce Him (the God who has the power to create the entire universe) to a vengeful and angry deity, waiting to punish the sin of one person out of the 7 billion currently on earth. The truth is, God sent His son Jesus to pay for those sins so we would no longer have to be punished for them. And interestingly, when Jesus died God also experienced grief because of the loss of His only begotten son. That's why God chose to use His goodness, not his wrath, not grief, and not the pain of loss, to lead us to repentance (Romans 2:4).

God understands our grief and in these daily devotionals, you can hear Him speak to you through the voice of Beverly. He gave her comfort, and she shares her comfort beautifully in these pages. In the end, peace and comfort do overcome grief, and I can tell you as she does, it really is going to be okay; you will stand on the other side of it.

Bishop Feb Idahosa, - August 2019
President, Benson Idahosa University.

Beverly stood on one side as I stood on the other side of her father, both of us holding his hands as he passed on to glory. When adults loose a parent they are expected to pick up and carry on with life despite the heartache, void and feelings of grief and loss. It has not been easy for Beverly but she has held on to her heavenly Father and through it all she has been able to smile. She has reached a place where she can joke about her dad and have a hearty laugh. She has learnt to depend upon her heavenly father. This book is an encouragement to those of you who can identify with her loss. May God bless and lift you up with His love as you read it.

Tabitha Dalizu Chahonyo
Beverly's Mummy.

Beverly's vulnerability and bravery in allowing us to walk her season of grief alongside her has created a gift of powerful reflections which connects us to our own grief, gives us permission to sit with our own tears and ultimately shows us a path of healing.

Most importantly "Hugs from my Father" is a love letter to those visible and invisible warriors who hold each of us on this most difficult of journeys and connect us back to love, hope and purpose. For each of you warriors, including Beverly…Asante Sana

Rachael Bayliss
Creative Director, Chrysalis Consult

◇◇◇◇◇◇◇◇◇◇

My sister, friend, co-creator, accountability partner, birthing partner, legacy building partner, voice note queen and so much more. I am incredibly proud of you on a number of fronts. But let me first express my gratitude for according me the honour to share my reflections on this amazing book.

A cursory glance of the book literally made my heart well up with tears, immense pleasure and a great sense of fulfillment that alas, the very book that will liberate and transcend generations has been birthed. I can only imagine how proud your father is right now and of course your mum and siblings.

The description of each day resonated deeply with me and brought back memories of my own grief, loss and the ever-present fear I faced having lost both my parents in a short space of time.

But oh! What joy to read your message of God's unconditional love for me. As I turned each page, I felt a warm touch of the Father assuring me that He is right by my side every step of the way. He indeed is a light unto my path, and for this, I am eternally grateful.

Psalm 23 came to life more than ever. I am free and have the permission to strip all the layers of hurt, pain and regret of maybe I could have done more to prevent my own loss. Thank you!

I'm accepting of the fact that it's very okay not to be okay. Cry, laugh, shout, dance it's all okay.

Thank you for this awesome treasure. I know it will bring healing, joy, hope and courage to everyone who has or will at some point in time embark on this journey of loss just as it did me.

God bless you.

Kemi Oye
Head of Startegic HR & OD at NHS England & Improvement.

Introduction

On the 25th of June 2018, in a quiet hospital in Nairobi (Kenya), my father took his last breath as I looked on and heard my heart breaking into a million little pieces. I was so hurt, so wounded, so tired, so hopeless that I never thought anything good would come out of his passing. Three years later, I look back in awe.

This book will take you through the little miracles I encountered in the following days, weeks, months, and years that showed me that his love for me did not stop the moment he gained his angel wings. It will take you through my good days, my ugly days, my God days, and everything in between.

I didn't set out to write a book. I set out to vent my frustration and document my pain in my journal because that's how I speak to God. Through my journals. But here we are, three years later with a book.

Words have always been my best friend. You see, with words I can create a world into which I can escape. With words I can reach hearts and touch souls. With words I can build up or break down. With words I can be whoever I want to be – but most importantly, with words I can paint the real picture of who God intended me to be. Small wonder that when I was in my deepest, darkest valley, I turned to words. Because words I can understand and control – people, I felt I couldn't.

My Daddy was unwell for a while before he passed. And in that time, I saw the different faces of people. Once again, the good, the bad, the ugly and the God. After his passing, I saw this even more vividly – and in some instances I didn't know what to do with what I saw. And so, I receded into my world and embraced my words.

Grief is like a scorned and vengeful lover. The harder you try to get away, the harder she entrenches herself into your being and refuses to let go. You need help to get through grief. Most people don't get help hence they don't address their grief. For me, after my words, grief counselling was the second-best thing I did for myself. It helped me vent. It allowed me to understand some of my behaviors and choices and why I did what I did. While it does not in any way excuse what I did during that season, it helped me to come to terms with it and decide how I wanted to deal with it.

To anyone I may have hurt during my season of tears – I am sorry. Forgive me.
To anyone who I felt may have hurt me – I forgive you and release you.
To anyone my story helped along the way – I'm glad that my tears helped wash away your sadness. Now please tell your story so that someone else can find their path to healing.

This book is neither an explanation of nor a guide through grief from the perspective of a certified professional. This book is me crying out through my season of sadness and telling you how God helped me to heal. I pray that this book helps everyone who comes across it and for those who need more, I pray that you get professional help from a therapist or a counsellor.

And finally, this book, my beloved words, my Daddy with wings and my Father in heaven helped me find my way back to healing. I'm still finding my way daily. But I am much better than I was yesterday and all the yesterdays along the way. I pray you find your way back to healing. Wherever you go, whatever you do, I pray you know this now and always: You are Loved. You are E.N.O.U.G.H.

Father Daddy Papa

I always understood the concept of God as a Father but never fully comprehended it until the loss of my Daddy.

Throughout this book you will hear references to Fatherhood. I recognize that it can sometimes become confusing so here's a breakdown:

When you come across Daddy, Daddy in heaven or Papa, that refers to my biological earthly father who is now in heaven.

When you come across Father in Heaven then in this instance I am referring to the God I know, love and serve. The one named Jehovah or Yahweh.

A Journey Of Love, Loss, Healing And Reconciliation

On the 25th of June 2018 at approximately 1800hours, my life changed completely. My heart shattered into a trillion little pieces as my father, my daddy, my first love, my covering, my friend, took his last breath and ascended into heaven. Today (21st July 2018) marks less than a month since he gained his angel wings. I say with confidence that he gained his angel wings because I know that he loved and feared the Lord and had accepted Jesus Christ as his Lord and Savior. I say it also because the moment he took that last breath a smile settled upon his face and he was at peace. I say it because in my heart of hearts I know that the Holy Spirit was confirming to me that he was okay. The grace, strength, comfort and courage I have experienced this past month has been something that can only come from above.

My Daddy always wanted me to write a book - to publish any and all of the books I had written over the years. In his absence here on earth I choose to honor his legacy by penning my thoughts, prayers and feelings into a 31-day-devotional. I won't write about how to overcome grief. Heaven knows that my heart is still shattered in a trillion little pieces, and continues to shatter every morning when I wake up and realize that he really is gone. No, I won't pretend to be an expert on how to overcome grief or how to mourn. But this one thing I know: When our Father in heaven tells us that He is the Father to the fatherless or that

He is close to the brokenhearted, I experienced that in this past month and continue to. For that I can only bless His name. Hence, Hugs From The Father was birthed. That's what this is about. That though my heart is broken, yet I will still praise Him because regardless, my God is a good, good Father. That's who He is. Nothing, not even this can take that away from me. Join me on this journey as I explore this new season - one that I never asked for, but one through which I have received a Hug from my Father in Heaven every single day. Maybe, just maybe, one person will be encouraged and if that's all this achieves, I will be at peace. This book does not only refer to my Daddy who went to be with the Lord, more so to my Papa in Heaven, my Maker and Savior who was always there, and immediately took up that mantle to cover me and be the Father to the fatherless.

1

REFLECTIONS OF SEASONS GONE: HOW BITTER SWEET

The seasons in Kenya are such that July is our coldest month of the year. That, combined with Climate Change means that temperatures in the past few years have been known to drop to as low as 5 degrees Celsius (41 degrees Fahrenheit). I personally am a tropical being both inside and out i.e. I don't thrive in the cold. I know it's a preference but I just don't like gloomy freezing temperatures. When I'm cold, I sometimes tend to be miserable. On this particular day, I woke up and rolled over in my bed refusing to draw back the curtains. I didn't want to see the dreary sky because it reflected my dreary disposition. Again, I realize that this is just a preference, a setting, a learned behavior which can be unlearned. I could simply choose to be happy - but on this particular day I didn't want to. I didn't have the strength to. I didn't have the desire to. I just couldn't do it, at least not in my own strength. So guess what God did for me, he sent me a hug from my Papa in heaven; and this is how it came. When I eventually (very fearfully and grouchily) peeked out of the window, the sun was out in all her splendor! The sky was an intense azure and the few clouds I could see were fluffy, playful, sparsely dotted across the sky and even inviting in some ways. The birds were flittering and fluttering away as they chirped and went about their busy ways, and it was an amazingly, pristinely, purely beautiful day. I cannot begin to tell you how that brought a smile to my face and tears to my eyes all at the same time. A smile because at least for today, I would only have to contend with the grey in my heart and not in the sky. A tear because I knew in an instant that God knew what I needed and had anticipated my every need for that day - way before the day had come. This entire show was Him telling me that while more days like this would come, He had already anticipated today and that He truly cared and had an answer. "Who is man that you are mindful of him or the son of man that you visit him…" (Psalm 8:4) came to life in an instant and just like that, I received a hug from my Daddy in Heaven and my heavenly Father. Sometimes He will surprise you, the sun will shine when you least expect it, and when you need it the most. In those moments, smile and bask in His love.

My message to you today

Grief and mourning can take everything out of you. On the days when you cannot see the sun, just close your eyes and feel the warmth from above. Sometimes it will come in the randomness of a blue sky, and sometimes in a friend coming to physically hug you. They say that just because the sun isn't shining doesn't mean it's not there. It may be stuck behind a cloud, but it is still the sun. Its radiance, brilliance, glow and warmth never change. Only our positions do. Today, this is to whoever is having a bad day: know this, the sun is still there. It is still shining, it is still brilliant and it is still warm. Don't trust your emotions, your eyes or your reasoning. Trust instead to believe in the identity of the sun. Its brilliance, its light, it's glow, its warmth. Right there, you will receive a Hug.

Father, even in this place of loss, pain and grief for (write the name of whomever or whatever it is you lost)---------------------------------, I ask that you allow the sun to shine on me in whichever way you see fit. Surprise me with your goodness and allow me to feel your love in a way that only I can understand because it touches a place that is raw and in need of healing for me alone. That way I will know it is you because right now Father, I need to hear from you.

Matthew 6:25-27

Here is the bottom line: do not worry about your life. Don't worry about what you will eat or what you will drink. Don't worry about how you clothe your body. Living is about more than merely eating, and the body is about more than dressing up. Look at the birds in the sky. They do not store food for winter. They don't plant gardens. They do not sow or reap—and yet, they are always fed because your heavenly Father feeds them. And you are even more precious to Him than a beautiful bird. If He looks after them, of course He will look after you. Worrying does not do any good; who here can claim to add even an hour to his life by worrying?

Today I Struggled With

(Write down the thing you are scared to say out loud or face. This will help give you the courage to face it)

....
....
....
....
....

Today I Overcame

(Write down even the smallest of things - they are all big wins and give us the courage to move forward).

....
....
....
....
....

(Make one commitment (however big or small) that will help you begin to heal. It could be - Tomorrow I will get out of bed or answer the phone or eat a meal or cry or journal or leave the house). Write it down and be intentional about it tomorrow, however hard it may look).

....
....
....
....
....

2

REFLECTIONS OF NEW BEGINNINGS: FINDING BEAUTY IN SADNESS

Exactly six days after I buried my father, I landed the job of my dreams. Let me break it down a little. I had always dreamed of working with this particular organization. I had wanted to work with them since I was in college. Since I was in college!!! At some point I had given up. Let me break it down some more, I started my freshman year in 1997 and I graduated with my MBA in 2002. My Daddy gained his angel wings on the 25th of June, 2018. So, when I say since I was in college, y'all need to give me a minute to do a jig and pinch myself because as you can see, it has been a hot minute between dreaming and the time I wrote this book. That you see, is the beautiful thing about God. He doesn't forget. While we may walk away or give up, He is still the God of the master plans. The God of favor. The God who does not sleep, neither does He slumber. The master strategist. The ultimate planner.

Over the years my Daddy and Mummy would encourage me to apply for jobs with this organization but with time I learned to "manage" them and manage my own expectations. That's what I told myself. The truth of the matter is that I was just managing my fear. You see, I feared applying because I feared being rejected, again, and again, and again. I don't wear rejection well. I can motivate the heck out of you and your situation but when it comes to taking my own advice, I am the absolutely worst patient. So, the week after I buried my beloved Daddy, the last thing I was thinking about was work, let alone working with this organization. The last thing I wanted to talk about was work - but here an opportunity presented itself. So I put on my 'big girl panties', I put on my big girl face beat, and held my head high as I tore myself away from my Mummy (this being the very last thing I wanted to do, borne out of fear of abandoning her and walking away from Daddy's final resting place) - but today we won't talk about those deeply seated fears that are birthed from the death of a loved one, because today is not about that. Today is about the hug I needed in this season, the one I never dared to dream about. Not only did I interview and get the job but within two weeks I had started working. You see, God's plans cannot be diverted, sabotaged or changed. They cannot be subverted. He is unchanging and His favor is undeniable. Jeremiah 29:11 tells us that He has plans to prosper us. Another translation of the Bible says that He has plans to bring us to an expected end. The end may be a surprise to us but nothing catches Him by surprise. It has now been a few weeks working there and I can honestly say that in spite of the tears and the heartache, my Father in heaven gifted me with a gift that my Daddy would have loved. Not just something to put a smile on my face, but something to keep me busy and keep me going through the dark days and the teary nights. He truly turned my mourning into dancing and gave me beauty for my ashes. For that, I am forever grateful. Don't get me wrong, a job can never replace my amazing Daddy, but a win is a win, regardless of when it comes.

My message to you today

So, I say this to that person out there who needs a hug from the Father today. His plans for you are unchanging. You may have stopped dreaming, but He has not forgotten the promises He made to you. His blessings are yeah and amen and everything you have need for, He has already anticipated. My dearest, know this: when you least expect it, He will come through in the most amazing way. My counsel to and desire for you is that you would not judge God's character by your dark season. He is a good, kind and loving Father. Weeping may endure for a night, but truly, your joy will come in the morning. And when it does, I cannot wait for you to write to me about it so that we can celebrate it together.

Prayer

Father I know you know my needs and my deepest desires. I also acknowledge that sometimes my desires are not what I need. I ask Lord for you to open a door for me in this season to cater to my needs while at the same time ministering to my desires. I want to be aligned with your will for my life and your plans for me. I open up my heart to receive from you even as you align my Spirit to recognize it when it comes.

Jeremiah 29:11

"For I know the plans I have for you," says the Eternal, "plans for peace, not for evil, to give you a future and a hope - never forget that.

Today I Struggled With

(Write down the thing you are scared to say out loud or face. This will help give you the courage to face it)

....
....
....
....
....

Today I Overcame

(Write down even the smallest of things - they are all big wins and give us the courage to move forward).

....
....
....
....
....

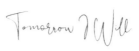

(Make one commitment (however big or small) that will help you begin to heal. It could be - Tomorrow I will get out of bed or answer the phone or eat a meal or cry or journal or leave the house). Write it down and be intentional about it tomorrow, however hard it may look).

....
....
....
....
....

3

REFLECTIONS OF FINDING THE JOY IN SAYING GOODBYE

Today let's talk about the joy of goodbye. My season of grief and mourning has taught me that this is one of life's biggest oxymorons. That notwithstanding, the joy of goodbye is a very real thing. Here's how it goes: I have heard heartbreaking stories of people who quarreled with a loved one, exchanged bitter words, made rash decisions, refused to turn back after being hurt and because that was their last interaction with their loved one, they have never forgiven themselves. An article I read recently talked about the death of a parent and the effects it has on adult children. It said that when that was the case, those left behind remained in the angry stage of grief for a long time. Some never recovered. It traumatized them for so long and that trauma became a big thing in their lives. The elephant in the room that they carried around with them. Some even died with that burden still weighing heavily on their hearts.

On the day my Daddy gained his angel wings, I was with him. I held his hand and watched him take his last breath. In that moment, I saw a peace come over him that I had not seen in many years. His lips formed into a half smile. His face relaxed in a way I could never have imagined. Let me pause and put a caveat right here. In that moment, my world shattered and I felt a pain that I cannot put into words. A pain that broke me, humbled me and reminded me of the many questions Job asked Yahweh as they were "reasoning together". It reminded me that despite how great we may feel as human beings, God is God and will remain God in everything He does. He will remain God above our tears, beyond our sorrow, beside our pain and around our brokenness. So, I am not telling a fairy tale when I speak. The pain was there and still is - it's been one month and four days since and that pain has not dulled, neither has it disappeared. I have my moments when a trigger will spark a well of tears. Conversely, I also have moments where I can genuinely laugh when I remember something about Daddy.

As I held his hand and he took his last breath, a certain peace enveloped my shattered heart. Here's why, I can genuinely say that I truly have no regrets when it comes to my relationship with my Daddy. He loved me deeply, and He knew I loved him intensely. I told him that every single day. Amongst my siblings, I am the Mushy one. The emotional one. I can cry at almost everything and in most moments. I wear my heart on my sleeve and I did so even with him. He knew I loved him, and just how much I loved him. I speak about holding his hand because it is a blessing and a privilege and an honor. It was the hardest thing I had ever had to do up until that day, and had I been given the choice beforehand, I may have tried to wiggle out of it. But that's where the gift in the goodbye comes in.

I lived in the United States for a few years while I went to college. I was in Florida, for a good four of those years and I saw a lot of elderly folk living there and dying there - alone. The saddest thing in my mind is for someone to die alone. Unloved. Worse still, with strangers when there are people – family, friends, loved ones who could have been with them. My Mummy and my Auntie were there with my Daddy and I sang and prayed and talked to him. I remember telling him that we were going to be okay. That he had fought so long for us, and the time had come for us to fight for him and for him to let go and to rest. I did this in between sobs, tears, numbness, a loss of words, nausea, sweaty palms, an intense cramping in my stomach, a splitting headache and blurred vision amidst the tears. I did it afraid, and worried about my darling Mummy. I kept looking at her and then at him and then I would walk away and come back again. But here's why I did it anyway. My Daddy was in my eyes, larger than life. He was my Superman and I was his baby girl. He was an amazing man. The magnitude of his love and kindness is felt more now in his absence. For the gift of him, I will be eternally grateful to God. I did it because something deep inside of me was confirming that he could hear us and he needed this in order to truly "rest in peace'. In that moment, the ability to be there and say goodbye, and the deep seated knowledge in the bowels of my soul that he knew that we were right there, that to me is the gift of goodbye. He did not die alone. He died surrounded in love. I have no regrets.

My message to you today

I write to you out there who has held a grudge with someone for so long that you forgot why you were angry. To you who was wronged beyond belief but has never received an apology. To you who betrayed someone so badly and have never known the way back to their heart. This is my counsel to you today: Life is fleeting. Emotions are fleeting. Memories are fleeting. But Love is forever. Make good memories today. Mend fences. Heal rifts. Apologize even if you were right. Live your life as though today was your last day. When you do that, you will be able to make memories - beautiful ones - and these memories will carry you through the days to come because each and every one of us will experience grief. Forgive yourself. Forgive others, seek forgiveness and live baggage free!

Prayer

Lord, you have told me in your word that in my anger I should not sin. In this season Lord, I am sensitive. I know that the heart is deceitful and also that I should guard my heart. Lord I know all this from a scriptural and logical point of view, but my heart and hurt are struggling to abide by that. Forgive me for where I have sinned. Help me to let go of past offences and hurts and help me to not offend or hurt anyone. Help me to hold onto you and I ask also that you hold me in your arms and set a guard around me. Like Moses, hide me in the cleft of the rock and when the time is right Lord, let me see your glory . I am weak and vulnerable. Be a shield and a fence and carry me through this with grace.

Psalms 3: 3-5

But You, Eternal One, wrap around me like an impenetrable shield. You give me glory and lift my eyes up to the heavens. I lift my voice to You, Eternal One, and You answer me from Your sacred heights. I lie down at night and fall asleep. I awake in the morning—healthy, strong, vibrant—because the Eternal supports me.

Today I Struggled With

(Write down the thing you are scared to say out loud or face. This will help give you the courage to face it)

....
....
....
....
....

Today I Overcame

(Write down even the smallest of things - they are all big wins and give us the courage to move forward).

....
....
....
....
....

(Make one commitment (however big or small) that will help you begin to heal. It could be - Tomorrow I will get out of bed or answer the phone or eat a meal or cry or journal or leave the house). Write it down and be intentional about it tomorrow, however hard it may look)...........

....
....
....
....
....

4

REFLECTIONS OF SAYING HELLO: THE OTHER FRANK

My daddy's name was Francis. We had many variations of it, the most popular of which was Franco. The day after I reported to my new job, a distinguished elderly gentleman walked into the space I share with my new colleagues. A jolly bunch. Always laughing. Ever diligent. They have been a blessing to me these past months. The gentleman introduced himself by both names. For the benefit of this story, we'll use only his first name which is Frank. That struck a chord in my heart, and I forced the chord to go mute. (I have since learnt that muting chords, emotions, actions and reactions is one of my most common coping mechanisms). I wasn't going to be the emotional new girl who falls apart on her second day. If you think about it, everyone has a defining moment in a new environment. I have always remembered people by those remarkable moments. Big Hair Don't Care, Super Fly, Wonder Woman, Power Suit, Killer Heels. Vomit Girl. Shaking Hands. It's a thing I do to help me remember and place people in my memory bank. It helps me to remember them and when I describe them to someone they say "oh yeah, that one!" So I was acutely aware that "emotional chick" or "crying girl" was not a way I wanted to be remembered. With Frank, his name reminded me of my darling Daddy. This only 5 days after burying him - and so I went into self-preservation mode. I quashed the tears, put on a brave smile, introduced myself by my first name, and quickly went back to being "busy new girl filling forms". A few moments later he went in to see my boss. She walked him out of her office not too long after that and stopped by my desk to introduce me. She didn't get far. Upon hearing my last name, he stopped her in her tracks. As it turns out, this Frank knew my Daddy Franco. It caught me completely off guard. He began to talk about him at great length and didn't stop - not even to take a breath. He went on and on for what seemed like an eternity but in reality was only a few minutes. He talked about his career, his big heart, his goodness. He went on and on and on and as he did, I slowly felt myself losing my composure and control. It is purely by the grace of God that I was able to stand my ground but I refused to give in to my tears.. I dug my heels in and willed the tears to not come.

He said the most amazing things about my Daddy. He wasn't saying them just to me, he was saying them to the entire office. He then shook my hand and promised to check in on me. It was a firm handshake. A parting shot before he walked away leaving me in a daze. I wanted to bask in the presence of the greatness that was my Daddy but couldn't take that moment because I was 100% sure I would need to take the day off if I did. I soldiered on and made it to the end of the day, and into my car where I wept uncontrollably as I drove home. My whimpers became sobs. The pain was too much. My wound was too fresh. I missed my Daddy so very much. A part of me is missing. But my Father in heaven decided to hug me that day by reminding me that Daddy really was special. Not just to me. He wanted me to know that He had heard my cry and that my pain touched Him deeply, but at the same time He wanted me to remember the gift that I had had in Daddy for 40 amazing years of my life.

My message to you today

You see sometimes in your pain and your grief, you will want to dwell on the one you lost. In those times, you may need to be reminded of the gift you had. A dear and cherished friend told me this a few days after Daddy had gone to heaven. She told me not to cry for the life he left behind, but instead to smile and laugh at the life he lived. Today, wherever you are, whatever you're going through, whatever you lost, laugh at the joy it brought even as you mourn and say goodbye for the loss you feel.

Prayer

Heavenly Father, I know that in this season I may want to dwell in the valley. Help me even here to see the beauty of you. Help me daily to recognize, acknowledge and share these gems as they will both encourage my soul and be a testimony to those around me. You tell me in the Bible that I overcome by the blood of the lamb and the words of my testimony. Help me to see these blessings and give me the courage to turn them into testimonies.

Ecclesiastes 3: 1 & 4

For everything that happens in life—there is a season, a right time for everything under heaven:
... A time to cry, a time to laugh; a time to mourn, a time to dance...

Today I Struggled With

(Write down the thing you are scared to say out loud or face. This will help give you the courage to face it)

....
....
....
....
....

Today I Overcame

(Write down even the smallest of things - they are all big wins and give us the courage to move forward).

....
....
....
....
....

(Make one commitment (however big or small) that will help you begin to heal. It could be - Tomorrow I will get out of bed or answer the phone or eat a meal or cry or journal or leave the house). Write it down and be intentional about it tomorrow, however hard it may look).

....
....
....
....
....

5

REFLECTIONS OF MY TRIBE

So I look around and I simply cannot stop marveling at how blessed I am. Let me just tell you, I have a squad of girlfriends who dropped everything to come and mourn with me. Those who couldn't be here physically called to cry with me. They didn't try to make the pain go away. They didn't brush it away with sayings like "time heals all wounds". They didn't get uncomfortable with my pain. They simply stopped everything and cried with me. They sent hugs, they sent prayers, they sent love, they sent love gifts and they sat in the middle of my grief and allowed me to completely break.

Those who were geographically closer simply dropped everything and camped by my side. They shopped, they cooked, they served, they cleaned, and they did all the things we couldn't do. They permitted me to crash and burn. They permitted me to be angry, confused, distraught, and hysterical and then they picked me up from my broken place and carried the full weight of my grief. They prayed for me. They drove me around. They made phone calls. They held me while I processed and struggled to make decisions. They even took my phone away and locked me in a room so I could sleep for 2 hours. They came with their babies. They showed up like nobody's business. They didn't judge, they didn't give advice. They just showed up, rolled their sleeves up and worked or sat with me in a puddle of my tears allowing me to be.

Some took time off work - and I mean weeks off - to be with me and drive me around and run errands on my behalf. One heard that I wanted to go to the funeral home for a private moment to say my goodbye. She didn't even ask my permission. That morning she was home by 8am. She ran errands with me, picked up two others, and the three of them held me while I cried, prayed with me while I prayed, then fed me, took my phone away and sent me to bed. In the midnight hours I can still call them. In the wee hours I can still cry with them. In the lighter moments I can still laugh with them. They never swept my pain away. They held me at the hospital or at home or during the church service. Some even got on planes and stood with me as we celebrated his life and later that day as we laid him to rest.

I have an amazing tribe. An amazing tribe! I will forever be grateful for you all. You know yourselves, and you will then be first to purchase this book to support me. You still check on me and spoil me and laugh with me and cry with me. I love you. You make my heart warm, and my world a yummy and fuzzy place.

My message to you today

It is in the darkest moments that you must find your safe place. It is only in your safe place that you will heal and rediscover you. The truth of the matter is that grief will alter some relationships and some may never recover. The truth of the matter is that after you're done fighting the great sadness, you may be forced to fight for friendships. The truth of the matter is that each and every one of us is different. What I have learned going through this is that while the world may keep on turning, it is imperative for you to not be angry with the world because it did not stop when you crashed. Look for who can be there (and the good ones will never need to be looked for), appreciate who cannot – and there may be some you never understand who will not, and move forward with those who are there. Most importantly, celebrate every single person for how they colored your world when all was bleak and grey. Appreciate them for their goodness and bless them for their unique gift in the season.

Prayer

Father I am immensely blessed by those you put in my life. Like the traveller on the road to Damascus, I ask that you show me the people for this season, the people who are in my life for a reason and what that reason is, and the people who are my tribe - those who are for a lifetime. I ask that you will bless them Lord immeasurably more than I ever could. Do for them all exceedingly and abundantly as you have promised. Bless them in a way that only you can - a way that I never could even if I tried.

Proverbs 27:9 [The Voice Translation]

The heart is delighted by the fragrance of oil and sweet perfumes, and in just the same way, the soul is sweetened by the wise counsel of a friend.

Today I Struggled With

(Write down the thing you are scared to say out loud or face. This will help give you the courage to face it)

....
....
....
....
....

Today I Overcame

(Write down even the smallest of things - they are all big wins and give us the courage to move forward).

....
....
....
....
....

(Make one commitment (however big or small) that will help you begin to heal. It could be - Tomorrow I will get out of bed or answer the phone or eat a meal or cry or journal or leave the house). Write it down and be intentional about it tomorrow, however hard it may look).

....
....
....
....
....

6

REFLECTIONS OF TEARS THAT FLOW FREELY

Grieving for my Daddy has been the hardest thing I have ever had to face. On the one hand, I truly am relieved that he is no longer in pain. That nothing can or ever will be able to bring him pain anymore. I am ecstatic because I know He is in heaven with my heavenly Father and that heaven rejoiced when he transitioned - the angels welcomed him with a shout and a bang.

But the pain down here is sometimes so deep. Today I celebrate the ability to cry freely whenever I must or need to. Tears are cathartic. They help wash away the sorrow and the darkness and leave you so spent that all you can do is sleep. And sleep is good because when you sleep, you can for those fleeting hours forget your sorrow. Sleep in this season can sometimes be elusive so my little two cents: whenever you feel the sleep creeping in, steal a few moments and lay your head down and rest. The brief interludes of rest are what physically keep you going and believe me, you need to keep going. Crying is the other thing that will allow you to keep going. Did I already say that it was cathartic? Well I'll say it again. Tears are cathartic. They help wash away the deep, heart breaking, gut wrenching sorrow and the abyss of darkness. They free you. That freedom to cry and the ability to do so may be found in the most unlikely of places.

An old man from my Daddy's village said the most profound thing to my brother and I one sad, sad morning. We had just landed in Kisumu City and were waiting in the cargo hold for my Daddy's casket to be released to us for his final journey to the home of his birth and youth where we would in two days lay him to rest in a beautiful ceremony. We were trying to keep it together. It is not an easy thing to do. As the plane landed at the Kisumu International Airport, and everyone disembarked, my family and I lingered. We waited until everyone had long disappeared off the runway. Waited until all the bags had been emptied off of the aircraft. Waited and watched as they carefully brought out the metal box carrying my Daddy and placed it on a trolley and drove away where we could no longer see it. We stood there and cried and just did not want to move. There are moments in this journey that marked a certain finality. Each moment was like a nail in a coffin or a spade-full of soil thudding against a casket. With each demarcating, debilitating moment, the curtain drew a little more signaling his final curtain call. When we finally got into the baggage claim area, the airport officials told us that they needed someone to come and identify the casket and the 'contents' therein. Basically, to confirm that it really was Daddy in there before they released him to us. I'll take a moment to digress here and say that the language of death is just as chilling and stabbing as the loss itself. Contents. Remains. Body. Widow. Cold, Cold words for a cold, cold thing. Death. So I accompanied my brother – we need a chapter on my brother, my hero, my friend. A dignified, strong, caring, thoughtful, meticulous young man who made us all so proud during that season. I love you to the moon and back! We walked into the cargo hold and watched as they unwrapped the casket and opened it up for us to identify him. He was there, still there, not going anywhere. Sleeping peacefully with a half-smile on his face from now until eternity. As we stood there feeling lost and hopeless and trying to be strong in the face of adversity, this old man from my Daddy's village said to us:

"Cry. Don't let anyone tell you to not cry. Don't let them tell you to be strong. He was your father and he was a great man. When you feel the tears coming, cry. Don't hold them back. Cry until you are ready to stop crying. That's the only way you will be able to deal and to heal." Those words released me to be me and to freely mourn my Daddy not only in that moment, but also in the days, weeks and moments to come. I would sometimes find myself sitting in my car, parked at a gas station (oddly enough, it always happened to be a gas station parking lot) crying hysterically. When I was done crying, I would drive on to whatever destination. I have sat in restaurants and cried openly, knowing that I was making other people uncomfortable but not caring because in that moment when the tears came, I stopped trying to make everyone feel good and succumbed to what I was feeling so that I could let it out and begin to heal. I have lain in my bed and cried. I have knelt at the altar in church and cried. I have sat behind my desk at work and cried. I have stood in the shower and cried. I have sat in front of a grief counsellor and cried. I cannot think of a single place I have not simply just let go and cried. And you know what? As hard as it is to just let go and cry until you feel your world has shattered, it is also in that shattering and brokenness that you begin to heal. Sometimes it is with tears in your eyes and a smile on your face as you remember the good times. Sometimes it is with anger in your heart and questions in your mind as you seek a way forward. Always, it ends up with me being completely spent, but also feeling a flicker of hope. Maybe tomorrow I won't cry so hard. Maybe I will. Either way, I live to cry another day.

Today I thank God for that old man's wise counsel and for the tears that flow freely. Crying is not a sign of weakness. It is a sure sign that you are alive and feeling and breathing, inasmuch as you don't want to or you don't feel like being here.

In the past two months, the tears have reduced - not the sadness, just the tears. I find myself having more good days than bad ones. I find myself embracing the teary ones as part of who I am and part of this process and season. Of this I am assured, my tears do not go unnoticed by God. He is painfully and painstakingly aware of each one. That gives me comfort. He never sleeps and never slumbers. He is the God of my tears, and the God of all comfort.

My message to you today

I want to encourage anyone out there who needed to hear this. Your tears will help you heal. One day, they will be a celebration and a memorial that you truly loved and were loved. They will not be wasted. And so, today, I give you permission to cry. Cry like a baby. Cry your ugly cry. Cry without inhibition. Cry alone. Cry with people. Just cry. It is a great sadness that you carry – and only a great many tears can free you to finally sleep. Be. Grow. Heal.

Prayer

Heavenly Father, thank you for the gift of tears. You tell me in your Word that even Jesus wept (John 11:35). Father thank you for allowing me the space to weep. Help me where I hold back, to understand the healing power of my tears. You tell me in your Word that you collect each of my teardrops and they are recorded in your book. Help my tears not only to bring me healing Lord, but may they give freedom and healing to others who will hear my story. And as you promised, wipe them away and let them become a testimony that indeed weeping may endure for a night but joy comes in the morning.

Psalms 56:8 [The Voice Translation]

You have taken note of my journey through life, caught each of my tears in Your bottle. But God, are they not also blots on Your book?

Today I Struggled With

(Write down the thing you are scared to say out loud or face. This will help give you the courage to face it)

....
....
....
....
....

Today I Overcame

(Write down even the smallest of things - they are all big wins and give us the courage to move forward).

....
....
....
....
....

Tomorrow I Will

(Make one commitment (however big or mall) that will help you begin to heal. It could be - Tomorrow I will get out of bed or answer the phone or eat a meal or cry or journal or leave the house). Write it down and be intentional about it tomorrow, however hard it may look).

....
....
....
....
....

7

REFLECTIONS OF THE QUEEN: INTRODUCING MY AMAZING MUMMY

My mother, my queen, my friend, my mentor. She is in my opinion, the epitome of the Proverbs 31 Woman. She rises early, she is all prayed up. She covers, she protects, she upholds, she encourages, she admonishes in love, she disciplines, she defends, she expels wisdom. She loves, she laughs - and in this season she has cried many tears. Through it all, she continues to cling to her God whom she introduced me to at a very early age. The one she has led me to love and to serve through her example of who He is to her and how she has loved and served Him.

You see, my Daddy was sick for five years. For five years, I watched my Mummy take care of him, love him, protect him and through it all, respect him. I look around at the world today and everybody talking about R.E.S.P.E.C.T and how they will not stand for this or go for that. I watch women, both young and old exposing the nakedness of their husbands / boyfriends / men. I watch them uncovering their weaknesses and joining the world as it stones these men. I never once saw my mother in all my 40 years uncover my Daddy. Not in life and most definitely not in death. She was his best friend, his nurse, his confidant, his giggle partner and his helpmate in every sense of the word. She supported him and cheered him on through close to 5 decades of marriage and close to 6 decades of friendship through visions and decisions, some of which I am sure she may not have agreed with or seen the vision afar of or even liked. "The heart of her husband [did] safely trust in her, so that he [did] have no need of spoil. She [did] him good and not evil all the days of his [and her] life." (Proverbs 31:11)

In her tribute to him during that cold, wet and dreary Wednesday in July, she spoke of a friendship born in their childhood that spanned fifty eight years. In those decades, her love and admiration for him only grew. My father was a good man, and made all the greater by the amazing woman that is my mother. Even today, she still carries us and covers us and mothers us through our grief, though hers has been as deep as the ocean. Even today, she still continues to be that example of true love and ultimate respect. Perhaps one day she will write a book about her experiences. For today, I come to the throne of grace to say thank you Father for a mother like no other. In this season, she has been, is, and continues to be my perpetual ultimate daily Hug from the Father. I (and all her children) arise up, and call her blessed.

I love you my Mummy. Many daughters have done virtuously, but thou exceeds them all.

My message to you today

For anyone out there who has a mother or mother figure like mine, take the time today to hug her. She needs to know how loved and cherished she is. For anyone out there who hasn't talked to her mother in a while

- life truly is very short. Take the time to call her. Seek to reconcile. I know of many people whose mothers have passed on and the pain that they feel, even years after is indescribable.

Prayer

Father, Thank You for my Mummy and the mother figures in my life. Indeed, it is not easy for a mother to watch her children grieving even as she herself is grieving but Lord, you are the lifter up of our souls. You who is the husband to the widow and close to the broken hearted, draw her close to you even as you heal her pain and hurt and tears over the years for things I may never even know about. Bring into the lives of those who do not know this joy people who will show them the love of a mother, season in and season out. I ask also that you heal relationships between mothers and their children the world over.

Proverbs 31: 30

Charm can be deceptive and physical beauty will not last, but a woman who reveres the Eternal should be praised above all others.

Today I Struggled With

(Write down the thing you are scared to say out loud or face. This will help give you the courage to face it)

....
....
....
....
....

Today I Overcame

(Write down even the smallest of things - they are all big wins and give us the courage to move forward).

....
....
....
....
....

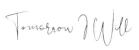

(Make one commitment (however big or small) that will help you begin to heal. It could be - Tomorrow I will get out of bed or answer the phone or eat a meal or cry or journal or leave the house). Write it down and be intentional about it tomorrow, however hard it may look).

....
....
....
....

8

REFLECTIONS OF BIRTHING IN THE MIDST OF MOURNING

One day I remembered someone, a dream midwife whom I had forgotten to call through all the chaos and tears and sadness. I called her but before I could say anything, we got to talking about her journey. You see this is someone whose seasons and cycles in her assignment are almost parallel to mine. When we are celebrating, we both are celebrating. When we are crying, we are both crying. And in my season season of birthing we were both birthing: one of us was doing so physically (by having a baby), and the other metaphorically (by writing a book.) Big things, historical things, monumental things, God things. She and her husband had entered my life and we had walked a tough season together. They had conceived and lost a baby pre-term. She understands loss and grief and mourning and doing it all while refusing to let go of the faith. She understands how to shut the world out because the world will not understand the instruction. She is an Elizabeth to me in so many ways. Whenever she approaches, the 'baby in my womb' leaps.

This past season while we had been praying for each other albeit from a distance, we had both been silently going through something. She had conceived and given birth to a beautiful little boy. A son of promise of whom it was spoken and for whom we had prayed and continue to thank God for. On this particular day, after we were done rejoicing over the manifestation of promise, I began to narrate my own path – that of my deepest darkest sadness. We sat on the phone for a long time as together we grieved over my loss. She cried deep tears. She was shaken. She was sad that she hadn't been there and sadder that it had now been months and I was only just telling her about it. She had met my Daddy on at least one occasion and his memory was vivid in her mind. She is a mid-wife to my dreams and through her this and many other books have been birthed. So that day as we related in this ship called life, she weeping for me and I rejoicing for her, she encouraged me to write - she encourages me still. And in that moment and through that process and in the months that followed that incubated and gestated this book, she prayed, pushed, reviewed, celebrated and saw me complete this labor of love that you are reading today. You see, nothing can be birthed until in essence, something has been laid down and died. You cannot produce unless you have laid something down. I had to say goodbye to Daddy in order for this book to come and once the book came, lives were and continue to be touched. This labor of love is the beauty that came out of the ashes of losing him. There are many others to follow, this is just the first of many. And all along, God had prepared a midwife in her and kept her waiting for such a time as this.

This book comes from a deep place of grief but out of that place is born something beautiful. Hope for tomorrow. Hope for someone else. Hope for the future. A decision to live my best life and give my best to honor one who was part of the best that I have ever encountered as well as the best part of me. A legend to me, my hero. Out of his parting, his legacy continues in me. I am his legacy. The words in this book and how they will impact lives are his continuing legacy. When a great one dies, we Africans have been known to say that a tree has fallen and the sound of it hitting the forest floor is loud. I pray that the sound of my Daddy's legacy reverberates around the world. Just as elephants stop and mourn one of their own and pay homage to losing one of their own, so this book will pay homage to the great man that he was and still is as he lives on through my mother, my sisters and brother, our spouses and children, and every single person he touched, Today, 30th of August (yes it has been two months and some days since he rested and I am truly standing only by His grace), I pay homage by saying this. Just as he fought for and protected us all his life, his departure leaves us not uncovered but protected and fought for by all of heaven's best – he being among them. Because he is gone, I can truly experience the comfort, love, provision and protection of my heavenly Father like never before. Yahweh has truly lifted me in these past two months and may this also pay homage and be a tribute to the beauty of the love I have felt and continue to feel from a Father who never sleeps and never slumbers. For me to fully experience that, my Daddy had to leave me.

My message to you today

Today I want to encourage anybody out there who has struggled with loss and wondered what good could ever come out of it. While you mourn your loss, take a moment if you can, to look around you. There is beauty in every single situation and every single day. You just simply have to open up your eyes and you will see it. For unless a seed falls to the ground and dies, it cannot produce the beauty of a flower. Therefore, in your season of winter, know that spring brings with it life. Know this also, no one thing, no one season is permanent. This too shall pass.

Father, in the death of a season there is always going to be a birthing. Give me the strength in this season of loss to push forth purpose. To birth destiny, to breathe life and to empower and impact within and beyond my circles. Help me Lord to birth legacy. I ask that as I obey, you enter into a covenant with me as you did with David. That my obedience will birth the promise of a future for my descendants for generations to come. For it is only in obedience that the greatest legacy is birthed. It is in obedience in the valley that the warrior emerges able to slay giants and flatten mountains - and so Lord as I walk in obedience, I ask that your promises will prevail over my children and my children's children for generations to come.

John 12:24
I tell you the truth: unless a grain of wheat is planted in the ground and dies, it remains a solitary seed. But when it is planted, it produces in death a great harvest.

Today I Struggled With

(Write down the thing you are scared to say out loud or face. This will help give you the courage to face it)

....
....
....
....
....

Today I Overcame

(Write down even the smallest of things - they are all big wins and give us the courage to move forward).

....
....
....
....
....

(Make one commitment (however big or small) that will help you begin to heal. It could be - Tomorrow I will get out of bed or answer the phone or eat a meal or cry or journal or leave the house). Write it down and be intentional about it tomorrow, however hard it may look).

....
....
....
....

9

REFLECTIONS OF MY COMMUNITY

I come from a very loud and boisterous family - both nuclear and extended. Over and above that, I have an amazing network of friends and an amazing supportive church-family as well. They say that your network determines your net worth and if that is true then I can honestly say that my net worth is beyond measure. Yesterday (30th August 2018), I received a message from someone who came to know my family over 30 years ago. She lived with us for a short spell before going back to her home country. We have hardly been in touch much over the past two or so decades but recently reconnected. She sent this to me yesterday: "I always admired how tender you father was with his "girls" (and [my brother] Sidney too). It was beautiful to see" Over the past two months I have heard repeatedly how many people were jealous, yes, that's the word that has been used repeatedly - jealous of my father's relationship with his children. This was throughout our childhood and, more shockingly, even while sitting in church at his memorial service, listening to us celebrate him even through our tears. He was gone, and some of their own fathers still live, and yet, they said that hearing us celebrate him only solidified the jealousy that they felt towards Daddy's relationship with his children.

From the moment Daddy fell ill over five years ago, until the moment we laid him to rest, and in the months since, our network swooped in and showed us the overwhelming love we needed. On the night he rested, over 50 people (yes, I said fifty) showed up at the hospital to hold us and cry with us. Over the next days, weeks and months, people showed up at the house, cooked, served, cleaned, loved on us, took care of us and drove us places. People showed up with food, and more food, and more food. At some point, we had over 40 loaves of bread a day and it was so much that we had to start giving it out daily to a local children's home. We had so much food left over that it sustained us for a few weeks even after the funeral. The dry goods lasted us months, I kid you not. My network, our network of amazing cousins, aunties and uncles stepped in, formed a committee, organized the funeral selflessly and did not rest until we had finally laid my Daddy to rest. Friends and family alike came together and just held us while we wept. They wept with us and stood in the gap for us in prayer and in love. Even until today we still have so much love and support. People calling to check up on us, coming to visit, hug us and forming prayer chains around us. Our network and our net worth truly are immeasurable.

My message to you today

Today I speak to those people out there who don't have a network as strong as ours and I extend a hand in love to you. My email address is **hugsfromthefatherthebook@gmail.com** . Reach out to me, I will walk with you through your storm, grief and loss. I will hold your hand so that you don't have to do it alone; I will do so by praying with you and for you, lending a listening ear, a helping hand or a shoulder to cry on. My network strengthened me so that I could in turn strengthen and encourage you. Know this, You Are Loved! Our heavenly Father loves you intently and immensely. He sent me to you today so that you would know that you are special in His eyes and in His heart. He has not forgotten you. He will never leave you nor forsake you. He never sleeps, and never slumbers. You are his beloved. Nothing catches Him by surprise. So today and always, I pray that you will lean into Him and let His love wipe away your tears and ease your heavy burden. I will be your network and you will not be alone. You are beautiful to me and your tears are only the beginning of your story. All my love to you in this season.

Prayer

Father thank you for my community (church, family, friends, colleagues, even strangers who reached out). Bless each and every one of them Lord. May this season in my life bring forth the ability to comfort others in their season of grief and loss. Give me the courage to reach out, the boldness to speak out and the wisdom to know how to do it. Bring forth the people you have assigned to me and assign me to those who have nobody but need a hug from the Father. Lock out selfishness in this season that I may give without reservation. May that giving birth hope in the hopeless and life in those who have given up.

Ecclesiastes 4:9-10
9 Two are better than one because a good return comes when two work together. 10 If one of them falls, the other can help him up. But who will help the pitiful person who falls down alone?

Today I Struggled With

(Write down the thing you are scared to say out loud or face. This will help give you the courage to face it)

....
....
....
....
....

Today I Overcame

(Write down even the smallest of things - they are all big wins and give us the courage to move forward)

....
....
....
....
....

(Make one commitment (however big or small) that will help you begin to heal. It could be - Tomorrow I will get out of bed or answer the phone or eat a meal or cry or journal or leave the house). Write it down and be intentional about it tomorrow, however hard it may look).

……………………………………………………………………………………………
……………………………………………………………………………………………
……………………………………………………………………………………………
……………………………………………………………………………………………
……………………………………………………………………………………………

10

REFLECTIONS OF APPLE CRUMBLE AND COFFEE MEMORIES

The hardest part about death is living in the aftermath. It is akin to enduring the aftershock of a devastating earthquake. Every time you think you are stable and things can go back to normal, something happens and you are once again shaken to your core. The entire world moves on and keeps revolving while you are left in this chasm of deep grief. This abyss of hopelessness. One day I woke up and realized that new memories were being created - without my beloved Daddy. It was the most painful thing in the world while at the same time being almost a relief. You see, not matter how painful the season, short of crawling into the grave with your beloved, you wake up one day and find that life is going on and that the okay days added to the good days outnumber the deepest darkest night(s). Initially you feel so much guilt. This, I came to learn, is part of the process of grief. Something similar to survivor's guilt. You may struggle to be miserable, or struggle to not be happy but you find yourself laughing and smiling and even celebrating moments and people as the days go by.

One of the things that helped me get through the early days was my new job. That combined with church and my responsibilities there gave me the courage to wake up daily and gave me something to look forward to. Believe you me that was by far the best thing that had happened. I didn't even know how much I needed it until much, much later. I realized that the week was well catered for, but quickly learned that the weekends left me listless, sad and desolate. One Sunday afternoon, I gathered myself and my darling mother and we went for a ride around the city. Then the week after that we did the same but stopped for coffee and pastries. Sometimes during our drives we would sit in the car and cry but always we would get out of the house and make a point of enjoying one another's company and reliving the memories whether happy or sad. Just like that I realized that when God says He has a plan for you it means that your life has a forward moving trajectory and will not stagnate. He has a plan to hold your hand and walk through the valley of the shadow of death with you. Sometimes, when you are completely beside yourself, He has a plan to carry you through the valley to the other side. He is the God of the mountain top just as much as He is the God of the valley. Always as the earth keeps spinning, He will carry you through even as He allows you to smile through the rain and sing in the valley.

My message to you today

My encouragement today is to whoever is out there sitting in the valley and wondering if it will ever end. Some days will be harder and some days easier. Some days you will cry until you want to die and some days you will laugh until you can't breathe. The truth is that nobody has a formula for grief or loss and there is no pill or prescription that can take it away. Allow yourself to feel the grief as intensely as you allow yourself to feel the joy of new memories. Don't bury yourself with that lost job or broken relationship or buried Daddy. Our Papa would not want you to be in that place forever. Allow yourself to grow, to live, to laugh and to love.

Prayer

Heavenly Father, today I make a decision that I want to transcend and transform from this place where I am to the place where you are. You are the beginning even as you are the end. For what I see is you standing at the place I am walking to. Lord, it looks and feels to me like my end, but I want to declare to my heart even as my mind accepts, that where you are is really only the beginning of what you want to do with, for and through me. Therefore, what I see as the end to me is but the beginning of who I truly am supposed to be. I am supposed to be completely transformed into I Am. Transform me Father. I surrender to the journey in your hands. I do not have the strength to do anything and I ask that you will do what only you can do even as you lift the heaviness of this valley experience.

Isaiah 62: 2b - 5

And you will be called something new, something brand new, a name given by none other than the Eternal One. And you will be the crowning glory of the Eternal's power, a royal crown cradled in His palm and held aloft by your God for all to see. People won't talk about you anymore using words like "forsaken" or "empty." Instead, you will be called "My delight" and the land around you "Married," because the Eternal is pleased with you and has bound Himself to your land. As a young man marries the woman he loves, so your sons will marry you, Jerusalem. As a groom takes joy in his bride, so your God will take joy in you.

Today I Struggled With

(Write down the thing you are scared to say out loud or face. This will help give you the courage to face it)

....
....
....
....
....

Today I Overcame

(Write down even the smallest of things - they are all big wins and give us the courage to move forward).

....
....
....
....
....

(Make one commitment (however big or small) that will help you begin to heal. It could be - Tomorrow I will get out of bed or answer the phone or eat a meal or cry or journal or leave the house). Write it down and be intentional about it tomorrow, however hard it may look).

....
....
....
....
....

11

REFLECTIONS OF HOW IT REALLY DOES TAKE A VILLAGE

Today is the 10th of September. Where did the time go? I blinked and looked up and the Kenyan winter was fast fading and our pretty summertime was shyly peeking and flirting with me. I love the sun. I truly love warm weather and I thrive in it. If you've ever seen a cat lazily basking in the sun, purring contentedly and licking its paws from time to time, that's what this warm weather does to me.

But I'm not just talking about the physical meteorological passing of winter and dawning of summer. Metaphorically speaking, the tears are still there and the heart is still heavy but God has allowed me to be able to find joy in the little day-to-day things and laughter in the most random places.

A few days ago some friends came over. One lost her mother when she was still a teenager, then her father a few years ago. The second one just lost her father this year. As my mother and I sat and reminisced with these two angels whom God had sent to make our hearts warm and fill our home with laughter, it occurred to me that just as it takes a village to raise a child, it also takes a village to mourn the loss of a loved one – be they young or old. Some people will come and help you cry, some people will come and organize things for you, some people will come and upset you with their well-meaning yet insensitive words, and others will make time after the fact to come and hug you in the stark silence of the aftermath of the burial.

The second thing that struck me is that as human beings, there is a tendency to gravitate to people who have lived through it. Only they can truly understand your pain, laughter, sarcasm and heartache. It was good to laugh with these two angels, to speak of difficult moments, how we had all navigated through them and still were despite the number of years in between our losses and that moment that lovely afternoon.

As I sit here and write this, another thought flitters across the recesses of my consciousness. You cannot set up camp in a cemetery and expect the fruitfulness of birthing. You see, grief and mourning are very self-centered emotions. The journey is personal and even as you go through it corporately, everyone's experience is unique. This one thing I know, the temptation to abide and dwell in the valley of the shadow is very real. So is the choice to one day get up, break camp, and begin to move - in any direction, just move.

So it is in life despite the uniqueness of your situation. That broken relationship, that lost opportunity, that job that has been lost, that father you are mourning, God has the ability to begin to sow seeds in your heart that will honor the gifting and consolidate your destiny and legacy. However, you have got to let Him. You simply have got to make the decision one day and break camp. For some people the decision comes easier than for others. For some people it is harder to find that place of peace and begin to hope again. For all of us, it is critical to your destiny for you to know when the day to break camp has come.

My message to you today

Today, I speak to anyone who has been wondering if it's okay to think again, feel again, love again, hope again. Break Camp and begin to move. The waters will not carry you, your enemies will not smite you and most importantly you will not be disloyal to your yesterday by living in today and hoping for tomorrow. Find your tribe, find your angels, work through your today so that you can prepare for your tomorrow.

Prayer

Lord, today I ask that you would speak to my heart and to my deepest sadness in a love language that I can understand. Show me where I have tarried in this place too long. And because I do not have the strength, neither do I possess the ability to move, I ask that you carry me and we begin to move in the direction of your choosing. I make this decision today to break camp. I let go of any guilt I have felt in the moments when I have actually lived since it happened. I let go of guilt because I know that guilt is not from you but is of the enemy. I am ready, prepare me mentally, emotionally spiritually and even physically. Like Joseph did when he was finally summoned by Pharaoh, I am metaphorically (and perhaps even physically) taking a bath, changing my clothes, shaving my hair and beard and moving forward. Have your way Lord. I love you. Where I may have trust issues, in this I truly do trust that you are in control.

1 Samuel 16:1

Eternal One (to Samuel): How long will you mourn over Saul? I have rejected him as king over My people Israel. Now take your horn, fill it with oil, and depart. I have selected a new king for Me from among the sons of Jesse of Bethlehem.

Today I Struggled With

(Write down the thing you are scared to say out loud or face. This will help give you the courage to face it)

....
....
....
....
....

Today I Overcame

(Write down even the smallest of things - they are all big wins and give us the courage to move forward)

....
....
....
....
....

(Make one commitment (however big or small) that will help you begin to heal. It could be - Tomorrow I will get out of bed or answer the phone or eat a meal or cry or journal or leave the house). Write it down and be intentional about it tomorrow, however hard it may look).

....
....
....
....
....

12

REFLECTIONS OF AMAZING GRACE AND AMAZING LOVE

So in this season, God is teaching me the true meaning of love or perhaps it is the meaning of true love. Love, I discovered a very long time ago, is not a noun but a verb. You can stand on a mountaintop and profess love until the cows come home but it is not until you show it in the way someone requires it that you will genuinely be loving right - loving the God way - loving God's way in God's love language, and spreading His love. I am learning patience - to be patient with myself and with those around me. I am learning not to take anyone at face value. Yes, that's what I said and that's what I mean and here is why - Just because you're having a bad day doesn't mean I should judge you based on that one encounter.

In the past two months I have come across stories of people going through real pain and carrying real grief and soldiering on in spite of it. In two instances, my initial encounter with the people was abrasive and aggressive and I did not understand what was wrong with them. I took it personally, "caught feelings" as Kenyans like to put it, and carried a burden of offence against the person. Surely, could they not perceive that I was in mourning and that I needed them to be gentle with me? You see when you are in mourning, your world is clouded with grief and every little single encounter with the outside world (even in its mere silence) serves to deepen your sense of entitlement in your grief.

I encountered these two strangers on my lonely journey of grief and pre-judged them for not perceiving and understanding my pain. Within a few weeks, God showed me the level of their pain and how deeply scarred their hearts were. Both were still grieving loved ones. One, her parents for over 40 years as she had been orphaned at the tender age of 10. She had never known what it was like to grow up loved because her step mother took over and she grew up unloved. The second one was still grieving her darling husband almost 5 years down the road and raising her darling children without the security and support of a husband. Their roads and mine, while parallel journeys, merged into one and our experiences, while unique, were also shared regardless of time and space. The former encouraged and prayed for me and smiled and hugged me through my tears. The latter is completely unaware that I was aware of her story. I pray that one day I will be able to hug her and tell her I See You! You see grief, of any kind just needs someone to see you. Your heart needs to know that you are loved, to know that it is okay to be where you are right now and to hear that one day you will no longer be where you are, and that too is okay.

My Daddy who went to heaven, you see, was a very loving man. He would literally give the shirt off his back to ensure that another did not go naked. He would empty his pockets to ensure others did not sleep hungry. He clothed many, fed many, built houses for many widows and educated many orphaned children. He gave his all towards us as his family. He would have given his life if he needed to for us - and I'm sure in a way He did. A lot of the things I have described in this book are because he is no longer with us. In death, he is still teaching lessons and giving trinkets of love. My inheritance as a child of God and as a Daddy's girl is simply love.

My message to you today

Today, as we journey on this road together, I want to encourage someone going through this journey of grief. I see you beloved. I See You. It's okay that you are where you are right now. It's going to be okay tomorrow. You are truly not alone. More than that, I want to encourage someone out there to let go of your tears long enough to see someone else, read their story and give them the hug they need today. Your journey will encourage others and give you strength - believe you me, you just need to begin speaking and God will do the rest. Today, this is my hug to you. I see you and I love you in spite of your situation. Whether still in a valley experience or conquering a mountaintop excursion, your pain means something to me and I am holding you dearly and hugging you - for myself and on behalf of our Father in Heaven.

Prayer

Father today as I send out hugs across the globe, I ask that you will open up the hearts of those who need the hugs so that they may be in a position to receive them. Sometimes we go through things that cause us to close up our hearts to love. Today I ask that you will heal anyone who has been hurt so badly that they have closed themselves off from the possibility of both giving and receiving love. Help them enough in this moment that this hug, this love, will transform them from the inside out to be able to not only receive, but also begin to give love. You are the God who is love. Teach us all our love languages and allow us to seek out the love languages of those around us, those in need, and those you have assigned to us, so that we may not only love them, but that we may love them right. Thank you for the privilege of being a tool to be used as your hands and feet. As I love on them and they love on others, bring people to love on me and more to love on them.

1 Corinthians 13:1-10
The Way of Love

What if I speak in the most elegant languages of people or in the exotic languages of the heavenly messengers, but I live without love? Well then, anything I say is like the clanging of brass or a crashing cymbal. What if I have the gift of prophecy, am blessed with knowledge and insight to all the mysteries, or what if my faith is strong enough to scoop a mountain from its bedrock, yet I live without love? If so, I am nothing. I could give all that I have to feed the poor, I could surrender my body to be burned as a martyr, but if I do not live in love, I gain nothing by my selfless acts.

Paul boils it all down for the believers in Corinth. Religious people often spend their time practicing rituals, projecting dogma, and going through routines that might look like Christianity on the outside but that lack the essential ingredient that brings all of it together—love! It is a loving God who birthed creation and now pursues a broken people in the most spectacular way. That same love must guide believers, so faith doesn't appear to be meaningless noise.

Love is patient; love is kind. Love isn't envious, doesn't boast, brag, or strut about. There's no arrogance in love; it's never rude, crude, or indecent—it's not self-absorbed. Love isn't easily upset. Love doesn't tally wrongs or celebrate injustice; but truth— yes, truth—is love's delight! Love puts up with anything and everything that comes along; it trusts, hopes, and endures no matter what. Love will never become obsolete. Now as for the prophetic gifts, they will not last; unknown languages will become silent, and the gift of knowledge will no longer be needed. Gifts of knowledge and prophecy are partial at best, at least for now, but when the perfection and fullness of God's kingdom arrive, all the parts will end.

Today I Struggled With

(Write down the thing you are scared to say out loud or face. This will help give you the courage to face it)

....
....
....
....
....

Today I Overcame

(Write down even the smallest of things - they are all big wins and give us the courage to move forward).

....
....
....
....
....

Tomorrow I Will

(Make one commitment (however big or small) that will help you begin to heal. It could be - Tomorrow I will get out of bed or answer the phone or eat a meal or cry or journal or leave the house). Write it down and be intentional about it tomorrow, however hard it may look).

....
....
....
....
....

13

REFLECTIONS OF COVERING OUR NAKEDNESS

It's interesting how quickly you discover your vulnerabilities once your covering is removed. A story is told of a rich and powerful emperor who loved new clothes. He cared nothing for his soldiers or his empire. One day two strangers came into town and promised him that they could make him the most colorful and amazing new clothes. They basically conned him into thinking that their clothes were amazing when in essence they were fabricating lies. They pretended to sew clothes out of "special" fabric (thin air) and they convinced him that the clothes were invisible to other people. To cut a long story short, the emperor walks around butt naked flossing all his wares, thinking that he was clothed in the latest regalia.

I started here because I wanted to let you know how vulnerable we are as human beings. The family unit defined by society today is so splintered: there is the traditional nuclear monogamous family, the single parent family, the blended family, the orphaned family, the polygamous family, the emancipated children, the estranged family and on and on and on. We have become so distorted as humanity that our notion of family has faded. Now our work family and our church family and our friends who are family replace the family unit as God intended it to be. And you never know how good you have it until you don't have it any more. I mentioned a few chapters ago how so many people looked at our family unit and our father and envied us. That does not mean that we are the perfect family.

In this season, every single day, my family and I wake up to a new reality where our covering as I have known it for 40 years and as my mother has known it for 46 is gone. I cannot begin to tell the story of my mother - hers is a longer one and maybe that will be our next book together. I can only tell my own reality. My Daddy was the person I called in the morning to tell him how I slept. The one who called me throughout the day to find out how my day was going, to give me traffic updates and weather updates (whichever was more important at that particular moment), to give counsel on political activities and current affairs. He was my political advisor, my philosophical advisor, my career coach, my financial advisor, my relationship advisor, my spiritual advisor, my friend advisor, my entertainment and my comic relief. We were friends my Daddy and I. And as I grieve this loss, I miss my friend every single day more and more. But more so and especially lately, I miss my covering. Today is the 19th of September. We are just days away from marking 3 months without my heart. Without our covering. In those three months, we have had petty thieves (mostly opportunistic ones) try to get into the house with one excuse or another. It's like they sensed our loss (or maybe even heard about it) and figured they would take advantage of the situation. You see I am the child who still lives at home. So right now, between my Mummy and I, the house is estrogen filled and that seems to be a scent that these unsavory individuals have caught on to.

When God says in Isaiah 62 that He has "set watchmen over your walls", He well and truly has. I recently went to report the above incidents at our local police station. As I sat down with a senior officer and recounted what had transpired, he at some point asked me my name.

The moment I told him my last name his eyes sparkled. He said he remembered my father. As he looked at me, he said that hearing my father's name and seeing my eyes, it suddenly dawned on him that I must be his daughter. You see I am the one among my five sisters who most resembles my father. In that moment, without being physically present, my Daddy had once again spoken for me and on my behalf even before I arrived. My covering was with me even at that point and Yahweh had truly set watchmen over our walls. The kindness that this gentleman showed me and the action that he took made me sure of two things:

a) God had made a provision for this very moment way before I could even have imagined it b) My Daddy was hugging me from heaven even before I knew he was - I just needed to hear it in that particular moment..

My message to you today

Today, I pray for each and every person feeling vulnerable and alone and uncovered, God has you. I encourage you to take a step in faith. Take a step forward. God has already provided a way in the wilderness. All you need to do is trust Him and step out in faith. May you find that covering when and where you need it but least expect it.

Dear Lord, your child is hurting and feeling vulnerable and exposed and alone and uncovered. Today I pray that you would speak for your child and cover him / her in this season. Where hurt, rejection, pain and loss has left them feeling vulnerable, I ask that you would bring someone / people into their lives to speak to into their situation in a way that is so acutely specific that they will have no doubt that it was you all along speaking to them. Send your angels (physical or spiritual) to speak on behalf of your child. You have said in your Word that you have given your angels charge over us. May these angels show up and show off. Father, show yourself strong for your child who needs this reassurance now more than ever. And may your peace that surpasses all human understanding envelope them. We speak against any unsavory characters who may want to oppress your child or take advantage of them. Run them off. And let your baby begin to feel safe again in your arms.

Isaiah 62:6

I have stationed watchmen on your walls, Jerusalem. Day and night, they never stop calling out. You, too, must not rest or grow silent; keep reminding the Eternal to watch over Jerusalem.

Today I Struggled With

(Write down the thing you are scared to say out loud or face. This will help give you the courage to face it)

....
....
....
....
....

Today I Overcame

(Write down even the smallest of things - they are all big wins and give us the courage to move forward).

....
....
....
....
....

(Make one commitment (however big or small) that will help you begin to heal. It could be - Tomorrow I will get out of bed or answer the phone or eat a meal or cry or journal or leave the house). Write it down and be intentional about it tomorrow, however hard it may look).

....
....
....
....
....

14

REFLECTIONS OF THE WELL THAT WON'T RUN DRY

Today has been a tough day for me. I can't tell you what the trigger was or when the downturn started but suddenly I found myself weeping uncontrollably as I drove home from work. When I think about it, it wasn't any one thing in particular - rather it was a series of seemingly unconnected little happenstances that orchestrated themselves into one moment after another throughout the day and eventually turned into an avalanche of emotions. I totally understand the saying "the straw that broke the camel's back". I have been holding back so many tears in so many ways because I feel that the moment I lose control, my entire existence as I have struggled to build it over the past three months will come tumbling down.

This month marks three months since my Daddy went to heaven. It also marks what would have been his 74th birthday. I miss him so dearly that sometimes I will myself not to think about him because doing so would break me all over again. Today I allowed myself to go there and the floodgates opened. It's funny how everything goes back to normal for everyone and in order to feel normal you force your emotions into a corner so that you can move forward otherwise the world leaves you behind. This is what I am learning and that is why today is about tears. I'm learning that tears heal. They help to wash away the hurt even if only for the moment - for the "just now" now you are facing. Sometimes they allow you to cry yourself to sleep because otherwise you would be awake hurting the whole night. Sometimes they give you a headache so you need to tend to that and it distracts you. Sometimes they just make you feel better in the moment until you can find a better moment. The better moments come, believe you me they do. Today, as hard as it is, I am grateful for the gift of tears. Because in a way, today, just for today, they helped me to remember my sweet Daddy and miss him without inhibition. Without judgment. Without making those in my world feel uncomfortable. They helped me to remember what I had lost and what I am missing in order to remember that he was oh so very special. Tonight, I am emotionally spent and therefore I will sleep deeply. My gift from the father today is my tears.

My message to you today

Today I want to encourage someone out there who wonders when the tears will stop. I want to tell you that it's okay to cry. I want to tell you not to feel guilty about crying. I want to encourage you that joy will come in the morning even if it might feel like that's too far to think about right now. And so, for today, it's okay to cry. You're not weak to weep. It's going to be okay. If nobody has ever told you this, I celebrate your tears and weep with you. I am in your corner and so is God. Our Father in heaven sees every tear and it does not return to Him void. Render unto Him your heart, your tears, your joy and your smile. Watch what He does with it in the next season of your life.

Whether you are weeping the loss of a special someone, a job, a house, a season, a relationship - whatever it is, just cry and know that this too shall pass.

Prayer

You are Fearfully and wonderfully made. God loves you with a jealous love. You are the apple of His eye. He will not let you fall. So rest your head on His shoulder and let Him carry you through today.

Father, today I pray that whoever is reading this will feel your love and that they will be reaffirmed through your love. May they see themselves only as you see them and may they rest in you knowing that your plans for them are good. May they accept your love and also receive love from you in the most amazing way.

Psalm 56:8
You have taken note of my journey through life, caught each of my tears in Your bottle.
But God, are they not also blots on Your book?

Today I Struggled With

(Write down the thing you are scared to say out loud or face. This will help give you the courage to face it)

....
....
....
....
....

Today I Overcame

(Write down even the smallest of things - they are all big wins and give us the courage to move forward).

....
....
....
....
....

(Make one commitment (however big or small) that will help you begin to heal. It could be - Tomorrow I will get out of bed or answer the phone or eat a meal or cry or journal or leave the house). Write it down and be intentional about it tomorrow, however hard it may look).

....
....
....
....
....

15

REFLECTIONS OF THE LAUGHTER I NEVER EXPECTED TO HEAR

Yesterday was a most amazing day. Most Saturdays come around and I have either filled them chock a block up with so many activities so that I don't feel anything, or I have left them completely blank so that all I do is contemplate and feel this emptiness. Yesterday was one of the former ones, but not quite how I had planned it. There is an old wise saying that goes something like, "…If you want to make God laugh, tell Him your plans…" So, I made plans. My girlfriends were coming to visit. They had been asking when they could come spend time with Mummy and I since we got back to Nairobi after burying Daddy.

Let me stop here and digress a little. Those words, burying Daddy - two little words that break my heart afresh every single time I say them. They don't get easier. They get harder because every time I say them, they solidify my new reality. A reality I never asked for, one I was never consulted about. One that ultimately meant my Daddy was better off but somehow in the midst of it all, it seemed like the rest of us were worse off. Let me right here and right now encourage someone out there. You are not alone. It's okay to not be okay. It's okay to smile to the world and cry in your private place. It's okay to feel confused, hurt and even angry at the process and the world. It's okay to question your Father in heaven because:

a) He knows your heart
b) He sees your tears
c) He says, "come let us reason together".
d) He loves you unconditionally.

Today is about the tough week I had been having and how my Father in Heaven and my Daddy who went to heaven gave me the biggest hug I have received in a while. You see when the loss and the death and the funeral were all fresh, the spontaneous miraculous angel-delivered hugs were almost common place. Three months in, maybe I am jaded. Perhaps I have stopped looking. Per chance I feel entitled. I don't know why but the grandiose romantic gestures didn't seem to be there so much - but yesterday, they were. My girlfriends came over. These girls have been my friends through distance and time, through vacuums of silence and chasms of words. Through weddings and babies. We may not talk every single day, but these girls showed up every time it mattered and yesterday they showed up – and it mattered. They brought with them lots and lots and lots and lots of laughter. Mummy, my Sister Milly and I sat back and laughed with Shaz, Marian and Cat and just couldn't stop laughing. The more we laughed, the more the lazy late afternoon sun shone through the windows and bathed us in her golden after glow. As they left, they left me warm and fuzzy and content. I was content, but God knew that I was not yet full. A few minutes later, my mother's Bishop, his wife, their Deputy Bishop and his wife (who also happen to be my uncle and aunt) walked in. Their kind words of wisdom, their laughter and joy, their prayers through these past months and this visit early on a Saturday evening have been a blessing bigger than I could ever describe. My cup was filled to the brim. However, God wasn't done yet. My niece, Carol, called as they were about to leave and walked in as they were driving out. She, her husband and their two amazing munchkins popped in, had dinner, regaled us with their childish antics (the children, not the parents) and then left. At that point, I was truly content and my cup was running over.

You see, I thought that I was going to get hugged only by my girlfriends that day, but God went ahead and brought a priestly covering and followed that up with an intimate hug from a dear one. And that, my dearest ones, is just what I needed to get through yesterday. I went to bed content and with my heart full.

My message to you today

To whoever is reading this today, may God send angels your way to fill your home and your heart with laughter, stories, a priestly covering and childish antics. May He send dear ones to minister to your dear heart. May today's hug be the biggest, most grandiose, sweeping romantic gesture to you today in the mighty name of Jesus! Be encouraged. God's not done with us yet.

Prayer

Father, I know that today there is someone out there who needs a literal hug. Father whether it be from an angel, or a friend, or a loved one, or a stranger, I ask that you send someone to their doorstep to physically hug them and bring love and laughter and warmth into their hearts and their homes. You created us to be social beings and not to live in isolation. So Father God, today, let someone from their social circle or someone you are sending to their social circle appear on their doorstep because your child needs it and because they need to see this miracle and feel this hug today. I am hugging them through my words and I know there will be testimonies of love and hugs spreading through seasons of grief and helping to lift the sadness and the heaviness. Thank you for my hugs and for using me to be a hug to someone else.

Psalm 98:3
He has been true to His promises; fresh in His mind is His unfailing love for all of Israel.
Even the ends of the earth have witnessed how our God saves.

Today I Struggled With

(Write down the thing you are scared to say out loud or face. This will help give you the courage to face it)

....
....
....
....
....

Today I Overcame

(Write down even the smallest of things - they are all big wins and give us the courage to move forward).

....
....
....
....
....

(Make one commitment (however small or big) that will help you begin to heal. It could be - Tomorrow I will get out of bed or answer the phone or eat a meal or cry or journal or leave the house). Write it down and be intentional about it tomorrow, however hard it may look).

....
....
....
....
....

16

REFLECTIONS OF BIRTHDAYS: ON EARTH AND IN HEAVEN

September 29th 2018. Daddy, today is your birthday. It has been a tough day. A very tough day. And it's only 9 in the morning. I have cried most of the night and even as I type this, I cannot stop myself. As I look around at all my siblings, my mother, myself, our world and our new reality, it is with completely mixed emotions. I am deeply saddened by the abyss that is left by your absence. But I am delighted at the thought of you in heaven and the gift of you while you were here with us.

This season has been full of so many firsts - so many things I wish I could share with you but cannot. Today, as we prepare to have your birthday lunch and be together, to celebrate you and to cling tight to one another in your memory. I celebrate you in the one way I know would make you proud - by writing.

You always took so much pleasure in my writing. You always took so much pride in my gift. You constantly asked me when I was going to publish a book. Over and over again for years you asked me that question. Daddy, I'm sad that you don't get to see it come to pass on this side of heaven but today as I type, you give me the strength to do it.
I have a story to tell you Daddy. Even from heaven you continue to be the wind beneath my wings and especially from there, your story con-

tinues to inspire people. Listen to this:

A few weeks ago, I was talking to one of my childhood friends. Let's call her S. We were catching up. You were always so fond of her, and she of you. She asked how I was doing. In filling her in on what the past few months have been like, I mentioned this book. I'm calling it my latest project. I told her about it and about how it is helping me to heal, one day at a time, one step at a time. Like you, she has always loved my writing and celebrated this gift. And like me, she lost her own Daddy not too long ago. As I recounted the journey and gave her an outline of this book, she was quiet at first and then began to ask very specific questions - not about the book, but about the publishing process. I was a little surprised but then again knowing how her curious and brilliant mind works, it should have made sense. We never got to finish that conversation (the challenge of technology and curse of dying phone batteries). The next morning, I woke up to this beautiful message from her:

> *"Bev,*
> *I want nothing more than for you to get your book*
> *(Hugs from my Father) and your passion to reach*
> *people through your word to come to fruition.*
> *You truly have a gift!"*

She sent me a love gift amounting to exactly 25% of the cost of our Project Daddy. Daddy, you are the gift that keeps on giving. So, thank you Daddy. Even in your absence, you continue to open doors.

Daddy, the story isn't over yet. So I immediately sent the entire amount to our publisher. I have learnt the importance of being faithful in little and how that grows the little into more. The next day, I was chatting with another friend. This is a new friend made in the past 3 years. She was checking up on me and asking how I was holding up. She knows how much I miss you and she prays for me - for us a lot. She speaks legacy and destiny and purpose a lot and she loves and continuously encourages me to write. And so it was that as we were catching up, I happened to mention our project, she went berserk (it's at this point that you would interject and ask me "Berserk"? No Daddy, she didn't really go crazy, she just got really excited. "So why not just say she was excited?" It's a figure of speech Daddy. Anyway listen …) She too decided she wanted to send a love gift towards this project:

> *Her: Amazing I knew you were a star!! Your book will be a blessing to many, me included.*
> *Me: Awww thanks love*
> *Me: Paid my down payment to the publisher this morning*
> *Her: Hahahaha excellent*
> *Her: Listen love, I meant to do this a couple of months ago, but the devil kept me busy. I want to sow in you, nothing much a little something, it comes from the heart. Can you give me your bank details.*
> *Her: And I will do it on Monday.*

Daddy, you won't believe it. She sent me exactly 25% of the publishing cost. Like honestly the project is 50% paid for and you and I both know that it's God financing this. I know you're looking down smiling. I'm no longer crying as I type because I keep thinking of everything you would say right now.

Daddy, you know how hard I have worked at publishing. Remember all the promises made by publishers, editors, publishing houses, false promises and broken promises. Remember all the quotations I have received, and my trying to make things work? Remember me meeting the amazing duo that is going to publish this book? All that and two manuscripts later, I still struggled with financing my books. Until now. Daddy, I think God wanted this to be my first published work and a living part of your legacy. This book is part of what you poured into me. This book is part of who you are. Daddy, you story didn't end when you gained your angel wings. Your story just began because your legacy continues.

So S's message and the seed she sowed, and N's message and the seed she sowed, Daddy you taught me the value of honoring people, the value of relationships, the value of sowing seed, and the value of hard work. This is by far the hardest project I have ever worked on but at the same time the most fulfilling. Today My Daddy, as you celebrate your birthday all the way over there, you are now and forever in our hearts. We weep because we miss you, but we also find ways to laugh because of who you were, who you are, who you will always be to us. Your humor, your laughter, the twinkle in your eye, your sweet tooth, your cheekiness, your passion for football, politics, and Afro Cinema. Daddy we miss you and today as we celebrate you, we do it with mixed emotions. Happy Birthday Daddy. Probably the happiest you have ever had because you're spending it in heaven.

Forever a Daddy's girl. Forever your girl.

My Message to you Today

There are going to be a lot of firsts from now moving forward. Most of them will not be easy to get through. Many of them will come with tears. Some of them will come with guilt. The temptation to experience all of them alone will be a great one. My advice, do so only if you have no other option. But if you have family or friends, a safe space you can step into to experience it together, then your strength will always be together and not in isolation. You are going to dread the moments, days, weeks or even months just before the first birthday, the first anniversary, the first this or the first that Only time can prove this to you but I promise, once it's gone, you'll be able to breathe just a little deeper. Go through the motions. Celebrate with tears or with laughter but go through it and get through it. Know that I am saying a special prayer for you in this book and that there are angels hugging you and wiping your precious tears. You Are Loved and You. Will. Be. okay. I promise.

Prayer

Dear Lord, I want to say thank you so much for how my Daddy loved me and how that love translated to the friendships in my life. He taught me how to love unreservedly and he taught me how to give unconditionally. I thank you today for the two angels who showed me the very love by sowing into this project that Daddy showed me every single day. Thank you for showing me that you truly are my provider and that when you speak a word of assignment, you will bring it to pass, be it by the hand of a friend, an angel, or a widow woman as in the Bible. I ask

Lord that you will confirm to someone reading this today that you truly have a purpose for their life and that you will bring angels to surround them and hold them up in their place of assignment. I pray that with that confirmation, you will also encourage them to not give up because their reason for being is someone else's only hope for tomorrow.

2 Corinthians 9:8
8 God is ready to overwhelm you with more blessings than you could ever imagine so that you'll always be taken care of in every way and you'll have more than enough to share.

Today I Struggled With

(Write down the thing you are scared to say out loud or face. This will help give you the courage to face it)

....
....
....
....
....

Today I Overcame

(Write down even the smallest of things - they are all big wins and give us the courage to move forward).

....
....
....
....
....

Tomorrow I Will

(Make one commitment (however big or small) that will help you begin to heal. It could be - Tomorrow I will get out of bed or answer the phone or eat a meal or cry or journal or leave the house). Write it down and be intentional about it tomorrow, however hard it may look).

....
....
....
....
....

17

REFLECTIONS OF LOVE FROM UNEXPECTED PLACES

Monday 8th October 2018. Today I dropped my darling mummy at the airport to catch a flight to spend the next month with my sister J and her amazing babies (let's be honest, they're not babies in the real sense of the word but they will always be my Babies). It just so happened that my mother, despite how much I pushed her, almost missed her flight. We got there just in time to be told the gate was closing. The young lady behind the counter (her name was Saida) was very kind to us - even as she chuckled gently at our playful banter (my mother's and mine). She checked her in and weighed her luggage only to find that my darling mother bless her heart and all her parts had over-packed and as such would need to pay the excess baggage fee. Enter more witty banter and Saida - the angel that she was, waived the fee for us. I asked her if she was doing it because she had a mother as cutely stubborn as mine. Her response shocked and silenced me all at the same time. She held my Mummy's hand and said: "I'm taking her to be my mom because my mom passed away in January of this year". Just like that, my heart froze and my tears welled up in my big brown eyes. The eyes I inherited from my Daddy. My heart breaks for Saida. I pause. My Mummy pauses. There is a silent understanding that Saida knows nothing about. My Mummy breaks the silence. "Saida," she says, "give me your number" she says "I'll be calling you because I have become your mother." I hold Saida's hand and tell her I know how she feels. My Daddy passed away in June. She looks at me and then at Mummy and you can see the recognition dawning in her pretty brown eyes. "I am so sorry. I know how it feels." She says.

In that moment, that fleeting moment to the world, I connected with a total stranger in a way that only grief can connect two strangers at an airport. Today I looked around my world and reached out to three very special ladies. One lost her Daddy two years ago to the very day and since I lost mine she has not stopped hugging me (virtually or physically) and telling me it's going to be okay. I have known her all my life. The second lost her Daddy a few weeks after I buried mine and is still navigating this animal called grief the best way she knows how. My grief is deep, hers is deeper still. I have known her most of my life. The third lost her Daddy a few weeks ago. She is near and dear to me the way only God can allow you to meet another person and your spirits connect and your souls tell tales as though they always knew one another. In the weeks following my Daddy's passing, she met me for coffee and I talked through my feelings with her. In the days following her Daddy's passing, she told me that a lot of the things I said that day never made sense - until now. Now as she navigates through the course of life and the course of grief, they make so much sense. I have known her less than a year but my soul and her soul are friends already.

Grief does one of two things. It will either drive you so far away from any person place or thing that reminds you of the great sadness, or it will inspire you and connect you with people who have been through similar things or people who walked you through your valley of the shadow of death. And sometimes, it will do both. Grief will either take so much out of you that it leaves you breathless and drained, or it will inspire you, pump you full of adrenaline and push you to live beyond your wildest dreams. Sometimes, it does both. Over the past 24hours, this grief journey, the silent companion that's been with me these past few months - she took my hand and led me to connect with one beautiful soul and then gave me the strength to reach out to three angelic beings and give them the hug they needed.

My message to you today

Today, I encourage you take a deep breath, open your heart, look around and pour out some love to someone who needs it. Someone who needs it more than you do. Someone who needs to hear that it's okay to cry. Someone who needs to know that it's okay to not be okay. Someone who needs to dig in so that someone else can hear their story and be encouraged. Today I dare you to step outside the comfort of your grief (because in it there is a strange melancholic solace) and be the wind in someone else's sails. The wind beneath someone else's wings.

Today I dare you to be the Hug from the Father that someone else needed to get in order to go through these next 24hours..

Prayer

Father, today we refuse to be victims and to allow grief to be our identity. Today we make the choice to stand tall and give strength to someone else. Today we make the conscious decision to pour love into someone else so that the sting of death and grief will not make us bitter. Today we ask for the strength to do better, to be better, to become better and to love better. Thank you for loving us enough to get us here. And thank you for trusting us enough to use us to show love to others. Direct us to the right person / people and speak through us the language of angels - love.

1 Thessalonians 5:11
So support one another. Keep building each other up as you have been doing.

Today I Struggled With

(Write down the thing you are scared to say out loud or face. This will help give you the courage to face it)

....
....
....
....
....

Today I Overcame

(Write down even the smallest of things - they are all big wins and give us the courage to move forward).

....
....
....
....
....

Tomorrow I Will

(Make one commitment (however big or small) that will help you begin to heal. It could be - Tomorrow I will get out of bed or answer the phone or eat a meal or cry or journal or leave the house). Write it down and be intentional about it tomorrow, however hard it may look).

....
....
....
....
....

18

REFLECTIONS OF TRIGGERS: GENESIS UNKNOWN

The past 48 hours have been super intense for me emotionally. I don't know what the trigger has been, most days I can't tell what the trigger is going to be, but anyway, here I am on Saturday evening sitting on a friend's couch and I cannot stop crying. She asked me how I was doing, and I gave her my standard "christianese" answer - not sure which one because I have several. She refused to take my answer and pushed and said, "No really, how are you coping? Because looking at you it's easy to assume that you're fine but I think we're rushing your healing". Dear, Sweet AM broke me with that one. I sat on her couch and cried for a while. Just cried and cried and cried and talked and cried and she let me.

You see my strategy in the past two months has been very simple. Keep myself so busy and laugh so hard that I don't have time to process how I feel. It's been a largely successful strategy if I dare say so myself. My days and weeks pretty much stumble into one another so much so that I can hardly blink before tomorrow is here and next week has come and the month has passed. However, God has a way of arresting you and on Saturday He did just that.

Fast forward to Monday evening and another friend asks, "Hey, how are you?" This one isn't even in the same country as I am and is asking via text and I completely break down. The most appropriate description I can give is that I became as messy as a bowl of spaghetti. I sat on my bed and cried and cried and cried. The thing about being too busy to feel is that it comes with its own set of complications. It means that I am also too busy to remember. Then it means that I am however not busy enough to feel guilty at not celebrating him and not thinking about him. Oh gosh, here go the waterworks again. The guilt builds up and adds to the exhaustion and the grief and one day the dam must break and because it's apparently such a huge dam, one day is not enough and neither are two. And here's how the conversation went with my dear friend KA - the one that had me weeping good tears as I finally took the time to remember for the first time in a long time.

> *I'm okay - for the most part*
>
> *Just miss my Daddy so so so much*
>
> *He prayed and blessed my day every single day*
>
> *Next week will be my first birthday without him - that's hard*
>
> *A friend of mine sat me down on Saturday and made me talk about him - I don't talk about him*
>
> *Kani*
>
> *It's too painful*
>
> *And then I feel guilty when I do that*
>
> *Because I loved him so much and he doesn't deserve to be forgotten like that*
>
> *Oh crap now I am crying*
>
> *Do you know it's the breaking that allows us to feel? And without the feeling, we don't taste the love*
>
> *Allow yourself break every now and then son you can enjoy the sweet feeling of love.*
>
> *I will remember that every single time i'm struggling not to lose control and break*

I remember my daddy's sweet smile and cheeky laughter. I remembered his wise words and look of disapproval when I did something silly. I remembered how loving and protective he was. I remembered how every single day he prayed and blessed me as I started my day. I remembered a lot of good things and I cry good tears - not guilty tears.

The dam needed to break y'all. As hard as it is to feel, I realize now it's harder to hold it in all the time.

We all need those people on our side who are able to break the dam while building us up and not tearing us down. We need those people who are not afraid to push because they know we need to get to our breaking point in order to be okay. We need people in our seasons who will sit and not judge, who will allow you to be all messy, have an ugly cry, love you still and keep your sacred things safe. These past few days, God sent me those people. So thank you to the two of you, thank you Lord and thank you Daddy - I know you're watching from above.

My Message to You Today

As long as you're still reading, I know that somehow this book is impacting you and touching you and for that I am grateful. I know that I have earned a level of trust with you in your journey. So today I ask you to trust me once more as I give you the simplest yet hardest of instructions in these two little words: LET GO. I know it seems like you're fine when you're "in control" but you're not. Your heart cannot control what you must feel. Your mind cannot control what you went through. Your control did not stop what happened. So let go, and let God. Let go and let the tears flow. Let go and feel again because trying not to feel is hurting you inside much more than you know. Let go in a safe space.

It's all going to be okay.

Prayer

Father, today I ask that you will allow whoever is reading this to find that safe space. That person, or place where they can cry without fear of judgment or intimidation. Allow them to let go of the control they feel they must have in order to get the healing you know they need that can only come through mourning. Help them to feel the release that comes from crying and help them to have happy moments and happy tears in that place of release. Bring them the right people and take away any toxic people who will bring them down or poison the process. Give them comfort as they seek you in this season and in this process of healing.

Psalms 107:19-20
In their distress, they called out to the Eternal, and He saved them from their misery. He gave the order and healed them and rescued them from certain death.

Today I Struggled With

(Write down the thing you are scared to say out loud or face. This will help give you the courage to face it)

……………………………………………………………………………………………
……………………………………………………………………………………………
……………………………………………………………………………………………
……………………………………………………………………………………………
……………………………………………………………………………………………

Today I Overcame

(Write down even the smallest of things - they are all big wins and give us the courage to move forward).

……………………………………………………………………………………………
……………………………………………………………………………………………
……………………………………………………………………………………………
……………………………………………………………………………………………
……………………………………………………………………………………………

(Make one commitment (however big or small) that will help you begin to heal. It could be - Tomorrow I will get out of bed or answer the phone or eat a meal or cry or journal or leave the house). Write it down and be intentional about it tomorrow, however hard it may look).

....
....
....
....
....

19

REFLECTIONS OF ANGELS ON EARTH

It's 4:35am and I cannot sleep. I'm sitting here thinking I need to do something constructive so here I go typing away when I should really be asleep.

Because of how early I leave the house (on a good day), I get to the office while the sun is still not fully up. That means I drive with my lights on until I get there and for the most part I have been good at not leaving them on all day. But not yesterday. Yesterday I walked to my car after a long day as the sun was setting and as I approached it I knew I was in trouble. My lights had been on all day and my car battery was flat. I didn't know where to begin. On days like these, I would have called my Daddy and asked him what to do. My siblings say I was "the baby." I talked to my Daddy about everything - from the littlest of things to the biggest and baddest. I mean it's not like he would have necessarily driven across town in the dark to rescue me - not in his latter years anyway, but he would have scolded me first then helped me find a solution then scolded me again once I got home. It's actually funny how he never let things like that go. He would scold you until you got it and would never do it again. He was my safety net and my solutions provider. He was my CNN (Chahonyo News Network) and my Google all rolled in one.

My daddy would call and tell me that it was raining, or that traffic was a mess, or something or the other was going on in my part of town so I needed to be off the streets and in the house pronto. How he knew half of these things baffles me to date - but I truly loved it.

Back to my dilemma. I called a friend and colleague but he had long left the compound where we work together. He told me to find the security officers and have them jump-start my car as long as I had my jumper cables with me. As I searched for them, I became frantic. Of course they were not in my trunk, and the conspiracy theorist in me started to wonder if someone could possibly have taken them out of my trunk – and to what end? I looked around wondering where to find a security officer and mentally prepared myself for the long walk to the main campus gate. As I did, I noticed a gentleman sitting in his car a few cars down from mine. He was sitting in the almost empty lot waiting to pick someone up. He had overheard my phone conversation and had already started coming over. Through his halfway rolled-down window he said to me "I knew you were in trouble the moment you walking out". [Who says that? If this was Conspiracy Theory Nut Bev, I'd have been replaying every episode of Criminal Minds I had ever watched and waiting for him to pounce]. He pulled up in front of me, jumped out complete with jumper cables, cranked up my car and then pulled back into his parking space and receded back into his world and out of mine like he had never been in it.

I don't know who he was waiting on or how long he had been there. I do know that God orchestrated his steps to be there just when I needed a rescue, because isn't that the God I serve? He tells me in the Bible that before I asked, he had already answered. (Isaiah 65:24)
My Daddy is gone, he's in heaven, but even from heaven he is watching out for me. "I knew you were in trouble the moment you walked out"

who says that? Who pulls up without being asked and helps and walks away just as simply as that? He may have come in the form of a man, but I truly believe that was the angel I needed yesterday. Just like that, I received my Hug from my Daddy and my heavenly Father for the day.

My message to you today

I want to encourage someone out there who needs to hear this. God is saying to you today: "I knew you were in trouble the moment you walked out". He already has a solution for you. It's going to be okay. He's already provided a way out from your seemingly hopeless situation. There's an angel waiting to rescue you. So breathe, Baby. Just breathe. It's going to be okay.

Prayer

Lord, these past few chapters have been what seems like a repetition of the same prayer and today is no different. Today I ask you to send an angel, in whatever form, to whoever is reading this and needs to know that you have already anticipated their situation, their pain, their dilemma and that you already have a solution for them. Father, you say that you are the friend to the friendless. The Father to the fatherless. There will be many situations along the way when we feel lost and don't know the way out. When we cannot see beyond what we lost. In those moments Lord, show yourself strong and prove to us all that truly our steps are pre-ordained and that you had the solution before we even knew we were in trouble.

Isaiah 65:24
I'll anticipate their prayers and respond before they know it; even as they speak, I will hear.

Today I Struggled With

(Write down the thing you are scared to say out loud or face. This will help give you the courage to face it)

....
....
....
....
....

Today I Overcame

(Write down even the smallest of things - they are all big wins and give us the courage to move forward).

....
....
....
....
....

Tomorrow I Will

(Make one commitment (however big or small) that will help you begin to heal. It could be - Tomorrow I will get out of bed or answer the phone or eat a meal or cry or journal or leave the house). Write it down and be intentional about it tomorrow, however hard it may look).

....
....
....
....
....

20

REFLECTIONS OF PURPLE BLOOMS AND CELEBRATING LIFE

So October is my birth month and I have always been known to celebrate in a big way. Not so much the past few years though. This year (2018), I made a decision to celebrate me the way my Daddy celebrated me every day he lived - in a big way! My Daddy always bought us flowers, chocolate and a teddy bear while we were in school / college. It didn't matter where in the world we were or what time zone we were in. He made sure it was special. He did it for Valentine's Day as well and he did it for my four sisters, my mother and myself as well. He taught me how to be treated – like a queen. And so to celebrate my birthday (and Lord knows I needed something to celebrate), I surrounded myself with love - because I am learning that love is the only way to heal. I surrounded myself with the love of my girlfriends in a safe environment. I fully expected it to be emotional and to cry a lot but laugh a lot as well. God, being who He is, surprised me very pleasantly. Not a tear was shed by me. It became a healing point not just for me, but for others as well. Sometimes we get so caught up in our fears and tears that we forget that those standing beside us are also fighting their own battles and nursing their own wounds. It was one of the most cathartic moments I have faced in this journey - not because I was allowed a safe place for me, but because it became a safe space for everyone who came and needed that safe space.

October is also the month of purple blooms in Nairobi. The Jacaranda tree blooms in all her glory and sprinkles both the ground and the sky with purple happiness. Usually I'll celebrate for all 31 days with my #31daysofwoohoo blog or vlog. I haven't done too good this year. So today I'll share a few words of wisdom from there one of my past blogs - I know it will encourage someone.

#31daysofwoohoo

Courage is fear under control. It doesn't matter how you feel. Do it Anyway. Do it scared, do it shaking, Do it wondering. Do it anyway. Only the brave break through. Only the brave stand out. Only the brave survive. Only the brave break through! Be brave…. Do it anyway

#31daysofwoohoo

For every time someone doubted, And every time someone laughed, And every time someone said no, and Every time someone ridiculed. For every one of those times, send them a thank you note. They were the stepping stone you needed to get to the next level. So thank them and move on!

#31daysofwoohoo

Rest – it's okay. The road ahead is long. You'll need the strength for where you're going. For now just

#31daysofwoohoo

Take time to reflect on the things
That matter, the people who care
and the places that mean
something. Take time to smell the
roses. Take a step back and
appreciate how blessed you are.
Know your tribe. Love your tribe.

#31daysofwoohoo

Live like there's no tomorrow.
Love
Like there's no hate. Laugh like
there's no sadness. Life is not a rehearsal….you only live once so get
it right the first time.

#31daysofwoohoo

The pain didn't break you, or kill
you,
or tear you apart. The pain made
you stronger, bolder, braver. Your
wounds became your scars and your
scars tell a story – your story. Your
story gave someone else a reason
to keep fighting – a reason to live.
That's your superpower! So don't
give up! Keep going. Keep fighting!
Keep swimming against the tide. You
are someone's hero!

#31daysofwoohoo

Don't let one persons bad behavior
ellicit a worse response from you.
Let it go.
Also there's 7 billion odd people to
choose from. You're spoilt for
choice.

My message to you today

For anyone out there who wanted a nice safe ordinary regular book when they bought this one and started reading it, surprise surprise, I'm not that kind of writer. I won't be safe or ordinary or regular but I will be real and this is as real as I can get right now. People are hurting. People out there in the world are broken and walking around like the broken dead. People in your life are hiding huge wounds and literally dying daily inside because they don't know how to get past the hurt. I pray that my words will comfort someone. Encourage someone. Move someone. Love on someone.

Prayer

Father, today I want to say thank you for every single person reading this book. I pray that you will guide them, be with them and even as you heal them, make them to lie down in green pastures, I pray that you will be with them in every way so that they too may become a green pasture where someone else can come and find rest, solace and healing. I pray for the grace for each and every person going through this season and looking for answers. As you comfort them, may they also become a source of comfort for others out there.

Psalms 119:76
Now let Your unfailing love be my comfort, in keeping with Your promise to Your servant.

Today I Struggled With

(Write down the thing you are scared to say out loud or face. This will help give you the courage to face it)

....
....
....
....
....

Today I Overcame

(Write down even the smallest of things - they are all big wins and give us the courage to move forward).

....
....
....
....
....

(Make one commitment (however big or small) that will help you begin to heal. It could be - Tomorrow I will get out of bed or answer the phone or eat a meal or cry or journal or leave the house). Write it down and be intentional about it tomorrow, however hard it may look).

....
....
....
....
....

21

REFLECTIONS OF THE POWER TO BE

Tuesday November 27th, 2018. It's been a while since I wrote. I am conflicted on so many levels. Without denying the goodness of the Lord, I must admit that these past two months, I have wrestled with this animal called grief. My Daddy's birthday came and went - the first without him. Then mine came and went - another first (I hate this season of firsts). Here we are, facing Christmas. I have gone through so many emotions - mainly anger. I can finally admit that I have been angry. At myself. At the world. At my Daddy. At God. I know there are some people out there who will judge me for saying that. The truth is, I just don't care. I have come to terms with the fact that since God is my Father, I can have a conversation with him where I ask difficult questions. Since I have questions and He has answers, if I'm not honest enough to own my anger, then there really is no authenticity in this relationship. I have been angry at people I thought should have been there. At people who tried to be there but "not in the right way" - it's not their fault really. It just is as it is. In a past life, I would probably have stopped right here to try and rationalize my emotions. I don't care to, so I will not. I have come to accept the truth that this journey won't be pleasant - not for me and not for many people around me. I have also come to the realization that if I am to survive, I must go through the valley of the shadow. I cannot go around it. I cannot jump over it, I cannot avoid it, I must go through it. The same applies even to the anger. I must face it and gor through it.

Anger, I had read in the past, (and have since come to understand), is one of the five stages of grief. It hits you like a tonne of bricks. It sucks the breath out of you. It drains your mind, body, soul and spirit. It makes you do crazy things. When you're all done, it forces you to withdraw from the world as you know it. When you finally emerge, you are tainted. You are bowed. You are battered and bruised. You are broken and spent. Just when you think you couldn't get any angrier, here comes another surge of anger. Your thoughts are not rational. Your actions even less so. You watch people get more uncomfortable in your presence. You want to reach out and welcome them in but you just don't have the energy to do so. Anger is a sacred place. You feel shame for the anger and yet, sometimes, you cannot control it. All you can do is lock it away in a deep, dark place and pray that it doesn't erupt in public. You feel like Bruce Wayne versus the Incredible Hulk - if you could just get to higher ground, somewhere isolated and wild, it would be safe to let it out. Yet holding it in is so exhausting, so you withdraw.

In this season, the hug I have received from my Father is in the form of those who have been brave enough to reach into that deep, dark, angry place, face the anger and not judge me. The ones who have said, "to hell with the awkwardness. I'm here for you." The ones who have said, "I will not let you recede into an alone place - I'm here for you." The ones who have known to come and sit and not say a word, just sit and listen as my rants turned to tears turned to whimpers, and faded to silence, yet still they sat with me. The few whose busy lives were never too busy to search me out for a hug and a giggle. Those who allowed me to be my new normal; not the bigger person, not the brave person, not the responsible person, not the politically correct person, not the humble mourner. To just be, without judging me and without trying to fix it. The gift to be and the ability to give yourself the permission to be, that right there, that is my gift from my Father above in this new season. I most definitely have more questions than answers (it's been five months and two days). I have more tears now than sunny days. I've just learned to mask them behind drawn curtains, closed doors, automatic (and sometimes plastic) smiles or worship. I have learned to put on my brave face for the world, then melt into a bowl of spaghetti in private, either by myself or in a safe space. I have learned to expect less of people (it puts less strain on relationships) and still to open the door to those who truly want in. I have learned that it is okay not to be okay.

My message to you today

Today, for anyone who is going through, anyone for whom anger has been or is a strange bedfellow, know this - It is natural to feel anger. It's what you do with it that makes the difference. So today, sit down and write yourself a letter giving yourself permission to be. Give those in your life permission to be as well. To be happy, to be concerned, to be aloof and awkward, to be distant, to be able to continue with life (yours stopped, theirs didn't). Finally, give them permission to be there for you if they can be or be free and without guilt if they cannot. I have learned that this life is not a dress rehearsal. You only get one chance to live it. I urge you to live life to the fullest. It shall come to pass that you will emerge different. Lighter, freer, happier even from this valley. In the meantime, guard your precious heart and your relationships. If they are to survive, you have got to be careful who enters your sacred space. They may not be bulletproof and that may end things. They may be tougher than nails and that will carry you through. Give yourself permission to be now, so that you can face whatever tomorrow brings. No shame, no guilt, no fear. Just be in the now, in the moment, and know that everything is going to be okay. Eventually. Because you just received a Hug from the Father.

> I sat with my anger long enough
> until she told me her real name
> Was grief.
> ~ unknown

Prayer

Father God, I pray for those going through the anger stage of this animal called grief. I pray that you will preserve their sanity. That you will preserve their safe space. That you will preserve their relationships and their friendships. That you will give them the strength to grieve without sinning. That you will hold them so close that even in their anger, they will not sin. Show them Lord how to channel that anger in the right direction and in the right ways. Help them Lord to focus their energy in such a way that they will not become enmeshed in negative habits such as drugs or alcohol or toxic relationships as they try to numb their pain. I pray that you will surround them with love and they will know for sure that they are loved in spite of it all. Father in this season when there is confusion and anger and they are emotionally unstable, I ask that you take a hold of them Lord, and guard their hearts and mouths for them. Lord, above it all, give them respite from the battle.

Ephesians 4:26 - 27

When you are angry, don't let it carry you into sin. Don't let the sun set with anger in your heart or 27 give the devil room to work.

Today I Struggled With

(Write down the thing you are scared to say out loud or face. This will help give you the courage to face it)

....
....
....
....
....

Today I Overcame

(Write down even the smallest of things - they are all big wins and give us the courage to move forward).

....
....
....
....
....

Tomorrow I Will

(Make one commitment (however big or small) that will help you begin to heal. It could be - Tomorrow I will get out of bed or answer the phone or eat a meal or cry or journal or leave the house). Write it down and be intentional about it tomorrow, however hard it may look).

....
....
....
....
....

22

REFLECTIONS OF GIVING OTHERS THE SPACE TO BE

Still on permission to be - I have realized along this journey, that as human beings (especially if you're as extroverted as I used to be), you will have expectations of those people around you. I have also come to the realization that those expectations can break you and crack relationships that you thought were solid. This journey is yours and yours alone. It can tend to get lonely, but the moment you own the process, and set people free, it liberates you in such an amazing way. The expectations we place on others are sometimes just too hard to achieve. They are too high and it can break you and break the other person.

I always wanted to be able to go through a valley season gracefully (when I was young I thought like a child). It was my idealistic thinking that broke me and hurt those around me during the process and for that I am sorry. At the same time, a dear friend told me that for me to apologize is for me to assume that I could have done better and that assumption is nullified by the fact that there is no manual for grief. There is no right or wrong and as you go along, you learn in the process - in the fire.

Grief is not graceful. It's not ladylike. It's not pretty. It's not well behaved. If you're not careful, you end up projecting your hurt, your frustration, your anger and your expectations on people who are novices in this - just like you are. If this is a first for me, it's definitely more than a first for those around me. Even as I circumnavigate this virgin territory, those around me are so lost in the process that they themselves don't even know how to breathe around me.

My message to you today

Today I want to speak to everyone who has been there for me, everyone who has tried to be there for me, everyone who has wanted to be there for me, everyone who has even avoided being there for me, today, I say asante sana. Thank you for your thoughts and prayers even when it was difficult.

Secondly, today, I give you permission to be. Be happy, be proud, be successful, be expectant, be ambitious, and be alive. Be whatever you need to be in this season. Just be! My promise to you is this. When I emerge at the end of this tunnel, I will be different. Because I will be different, I am sure you will be too. As we survey one another both now and later, I promise to remember I gave you permission to be and thus I will not hold it against you wherever you are along life's journey. I celebrate you in advance for where you will be and I salute you even now as I recognize your champion spirit in your tomorrow success. As you become that which you were always supposed to be, I give you permission to be who you were always meant to be to me. A rock, a foundation, a shoulder, a hug, a smile, a tear, a peal of laughter, a for now relationship, or a forever person. I love you for whom you have been to me. For now, I give you permission to be beautiful and amazing and wonderful to yourself always.

Lord, I come before you today, humbled by your unconditional love for me and your unmerited grace over my life especially through this season. I come to you asking you to forgive me where I have judged both myself and others harshly. I ask Lord that you mend relationships that may have been wounded in this season by my words, actions and thoughts. I ask that you heal and offer comfort to all those who mourned with me and all those who wanted to but did not have a chance. If there is anyone I have hurt (knowingly or un-knowingly), I ask for your forgiveness and for theirs. I ask that you will give me the courage and the wisdom to seek forgiveness and to find my place of peace even as they find theirs. Lord, I thank you for them. I celebrate them, their journey and their success. And finally Lord, for whoever is out there reading this, I pray that you touch them and heal them and give them the wisdom and the courage to give those around them the permission to be, and to let them go and heal.

Colossians 3:12 – 14

Since you are all set apart by God, made holy and dearly loved, clothe yourselves with a holy way of life: compassion, kindness, humility, gentleness, and patience. 13 Put up with one another. Forgive. Pardon any offenses against one another, as the Lord has pardoned you, because you should act in kind. 14 But above all these, put on love! Love is the perfect tie to bind these together.

Today I Struggled With

(Write down the thing you are scared to say out loud or face. This will help give you the courage to face it)

....
....
....
....
....

Today I Overcame

(Write down even the smallest of things - they are all big wins and give us the courage to move forward).

....
....
....
....
....

Tomorrow I Will

(Make one commitment (however big or small) that will help you begin to heal. It could be - Tomorrow I will get out of bed or answer the phone or eat a meal or cry or journal or leave the house). Write it down and be intentional about it tomorrow, however hard it may look).

....
....
....
....
....

23

REFLECTIONS OF THE FEAR OF FORGETTING

As I mentioned a few chapters back, I haven't written in a long time. Two months to be precise. Within those two months a lot has happened. Today I want to recap the harsh reality of panic attacks while on my grief journey. You see, for the longest time, I had developed and embraced the coping mechanism of just not facing the harsh reality of death - basically just avoiding the reality thereof altogether! Let me put that in a different way, in the aftermath of the harsh reality and bitter finality of my Daddy's death, I buried myself in work and in being busy. Two Bible Studies a week, work five days a week, catching up with friends and loved ones one day a week, shopping, bringing order, watching movies, being social (it was draining). And because it was so draining, I followed this grand act with another grand act. I isolated myself from the world and became a recluse. Honestly speaking, it took a huge toll on me.

The one thing I was avoiding was the thought of September 29th - it was fast approaching and I did not know how to deal with my Daddy's first birthday without him. I'm not sure I'll know how to deal with the second or third or any other for that matter, but this particular one, I was so scared of it. The fear of the unknown was crippling, it was so final. It was so very harsh and cruel that thinking about it literally paralyzed me with fear. One day I woke up and was desperate to find something, anything and everything that bound me to my Daddy. I was scared of forgetting him. I went to my phone to look for a text message, a trail, anything between me and him. Nothing. You see my phone had broken earlier in the year and it took me a while to fix it so I had nothing from the year he passed or anything prior to that. I had also done the "clever" thing and set the time limit for text messages to three months before being deleted permanently. I went through two different handsets and still couldn't find anything. As I faced the reality of not having anything to physically cling to him with, I panicked. I woke up in the middle of the night for three weeks in a row and desperately and erratically combed through my belongings to find something, anything. The more I looked, the more I didn't find anything and consequently the more desperate and fearful I got. Then one day I was driving home from work and it hit me, I don't have a text message, or a letter, or anything personal between me and him - nothing. I cracked. As I drove, I began to cry. The sorrow and the pain racked my body and I began to sob, then I began to scream. My screams were of anger, pain, confusion, regret and so many other emotions that I am not sure I have the strength to attempt to describe or to think about it. The fear gripped me continuously. I would find myself sweating and wondering if people noticed. My palms would shake uncontrollably. I would be in the middle of a conversation and my natural mind would wander into "I can't wait till the end of the day to tell Mummy and Daddy about this" and then I would stop and remember that I couldn't tell him anything. I would zone out and feel like I was being engulfed in a black abyss. I would find myself going to the car in the middle of the day to force myself to breathe. I had learned to hold my breath because I was gripped with the fear that I was going to "crack" in public. I was in a bad place and I did not know how to get out of it. I did not want to ask for help because surely months later I should be able to handle it. I was scared to speak to our staff counsellor at work because I was scared that it would impact on my new job. I was scared to talk to my Mummy because I didn't want to worry her any more - wasn't her grief deep enough already? I was scared to let the world see me crack because I did not want pity or to be weak. I was scared of disappointing Daddy. Scared of forgetting him. Scared of losing control. Scared of everything - just scared.

This went on for a while. And then one day, after the sadness, hopelessness and desperation had receded, it hit me. I am his daughter, I will always be. He is my father. He will always and eternally be. There is nothing that can take that away. There is a scripture that talks about how nothing can separate me from the love of God. It tells me that if I make my bed in hell, he will find me there. One day with the dawning of the day, just like that, it dawned on me. Nothing could ever separate me from the love of my earthly father. Not death, and not a message or the lack thereof. I am his baby girl and he will forever be my first Valentine. He was my loving father in life and will eternally be my loving father in heaven. While I may only have one message from years ago that I finally managed to salvage, he will always be a source of my strength and encouragement because of how he impacted me while he was here. I see his smile in every picture. I hear his I love you too when I close my eyes. The peace I know I have in my heart (from time to time) is all the confirmation I need that my Daddy's love and laughter and light will never, ever leave me. I did not lose a Father, I gained a guardian angel. He will always smile down on me and will always watch over me. In this celebration of his life and legacy, he will forever be etched in the hearts and minds of those who come across his memory and his life through this book. That right there is the best thing I could ever do to remember him. That right there is my hug from my father today - from both my Daddy in Heaven and my Father in Heaven.

My message to you today

I struggled to write the "message for you today" over the last few chapters. That's because sometimes I don't have a message. It doesn't come automatically. That is what grief looks like. Sometimes you will do things out of obligation and then a time will come when you decide that you need to take care of you and encouraging others is not a top priority. However this is my message to you out there today. The memories of your loved ones will never fade. You will love them as fiercely in 19 years as you did the day they left this earth. Their love for you will never fade either. It will be just as real 50 years from today. Take comfort in that and consider this your Hug From Your Father today.

Let me also make this very clear, I finally did have a conversation with our staff counsellor and he walked with me through some very difficult conversations including the one where he asked me to stop trying to control my grief and just allow myself to process it. Asking for help and hitting rock bottom is not a sign of weakness. It is actually a sign of strength. So please, my dearest loved ones, ask for help. It's okay to do so. Again, I am not an expert on grief or grief counsellor but if you ever need just to reach out and talk to someone, you can reach me on [insert email here] and I will listen and I will pray for you and I will help you get the help you need.

Prayer

Dear Lord, thank you for helping me through the anxiety and panic. Thank you for giving me a solid support system to carry me through this. I do not take it for granted. Today I pray for anyone out there who desperately needs help. Anyone going through anxiety and experiencing panic attacks. I ask God that your peace will envelop them and surround them. I also ask Lord that you will give them the boldness and courage to be strong enough to ask for help. Finally Lord, I ask for you to place the right people and resources around them to help them. Let them know that you love them even as I tell them that I love them and pray for them.

Philippians 4:6-7

Don't be anxious about things; instead, pray. Pray about everything. He longs to hear your requests, so talk to God about your needs and be thankful for what has come. 7 And know that the peace of God (a peace that is beyond any and all of our human understanding) will stand watch over your hearts and minds in Jesus, the Anointed One.

Today I Struggled With

(Write down the thing you are scared to say out loud or face. This will help give you the courage to face it)

....
....
....
....
....

Today I Overcame

(Write down even the smallest of things - they are all big wins and give us the courage to move forward).

....
....
....
....
....

Tomorrow I Will

(Make one commitment (however small or big) that will help you begin to heal. It could be - Tomorrow I will get out of bed or answer the phone or eat a meal or cry or journal or leave the house). Write it down and be intentional about it tomorrow, however hard it may look).

....
....
....
....
....

24

REFLECTIONS OF TIME STAMPS

The last three months have been different. Not different in that I feel his loss any less. Different in that I have realized that time helps. They say time heals all wounds. I'm sure the proverbial "they" have a reason why they say that - I am yet to prove it. I will therefore amend "their" saying to my own personal journey - "Time helps all hurts." You see, every single month for the past three months, I have not noticed the 25th day of the month. I have not stopped to break down and feel that suffocating fear tighten in my throat. I have not re-lived that day five months ago moment by moment. Now don't get me wrong, I may have done so on different days of the month and I may have done so multiple times in the same day and hundreds of times in the same month, but on the 25th day, God's grace has somehow covered me and I have somehow forgotten that that date (the 25th of every month) marks the day that my life changed forever.

My Bible tells me that God's grace is sufficient and His strength is made perfect in my weakness. (2 Corinthians 12:9-10). I like how The Message translation puts it: "My grace is enough. It's all you need. My strength comes into its own in your weakness." That verse right there is what I feel translates to this right here situation, in this right here season of my life. His grace covers me when I need covering. It blinds me to my deepest fear. It protects me from my darkest sorrow and it brings me to another day. A brighter day. A day to celebrate. A day to smile.

On the days when I cannot smile, where I cry uncontrollably, where I am broken beyond brokenness and where the darkness of sorrow and sadness threatens to overwhelm and suffocate me, in those moments and on those days, His strength perfects my weakness.

I looked up the dictionary definition of grace and it is described as smoothness and elegance of movement. That is exactly what I have experienced these past few months, and especially so on the 25th day of the month, every month - a smoothness and elegance of movement through the day. You see the Lord knows that I need to get through each month and through that day in each month in particular. Sometimes, He will step in and give me smoothness and elegance of movement through the day. Another meaning I found and loved is that Grace is the free and unmerited favor of God, as manifested in the salvation of sinners and the bestowal of blessings. I like the part that says free and unmerited favor of God. It is nondescript and indiscriminate. That applies not only to me as a person among 7 and a half billion odd others, but also to each and every situation I will ever face. God already has me covered.

My message to you today

Today, to anyone who is going through it, know this, even when you don't know it, feel it, want to acknowledge or feel you must control it, no matter your season, situation, circumstance or level of pain or grief, God's free and unmerited favor provides for a smoothness and elegant movement through the fire. I promise you this one thing; you will come out on the other side. It's important to go through. So go through knowing that as I sat here and poured my heart and tears into this book, it was just for you, and I prayed as I did it. Because of that, these words will permeate and allow you to cry or to smile or to breathe for the first time. They will give you hope because they have given me hope. When you do come out on the other side, it will be by the free and unmerited favor of the God whose strength is enough, whose strength is all that you will ever need. To help you go through today, here is a Hug from the Father.

Prayer

Father, today I thank you for your unmerited grace and favour on the good days and even on the tougher days. Thank you for the extra grace that you continue to pour out on me on the special days. The firsts, the favourites and even the dreaded days. Thank you Lord for carrying me when I couldn't even get past the thought of having to wake up, face the day and confront my grief. Today, I pray that everyone reading this book will experience your unmerited grace and favour in their season, in their battle, in their situation and in their reality. I thank you Lord that they are making progress even though they may not see it. I thank you that they are getting better at not being okay and that slowly but surely they are gaining the strength to accept their new reality. I pray that today your grace gives them something to celebrate in this journey.

Ephesians 4:7
This God has given to each of us grace in full measure according to the Anointed's gift

Today I Struggled With

(Write down the thing you are scared to say out loud or face. This will help give you the courage to face it)

....
....
....
....
....

Today I Overcame

(Write down even the smallest of things - they are all big wins and give us the courage to move forward).

....
....
....
....
....

(Make one commitment (however big or small) that will help you begin to heal. It could be - Tomorrow I will get out of bed or answer the phone or eat a meal or cry or journal or leave the house). Write it down and be intentional about it tomorrow, however hard it may look).

....
....
....
....
....

25

REFLECTIONS OF FRAGRANCES FROM MY CHILDHOOD

November of 2018, 5 months into this journey, and I had lost my desire to inspire. I didn't want to be inspirational and I didn't want to be inspired. I just wanted to be sad and angry and confused. There is a strange but familiar place in grief where the darker side is almost comforting. You want to cling to it, at least I did. Now when I started this book I said that I was not a grief counsellor or a professional and I was not writing a manual on how to go through grief, neither was I giving solutions. These are just my thoughts and feelings as I go through this journey. I acknowledge the fact that everybody's journey is going to be different. Some people will get out of each stage faster, while others will linger. Some will pass through with just the kindness of time, and others will need a little extra help. I know I did. I came to that stage and decided that it was easier to embrace the anger than to face the finality and reality that I don't have control over anything and there was nothing I could do about it. I stopped being social and receded into he darkness. It was familiar and strangely comforting. I didn't want to be around people. I withdrew from those who loved me, partly for fear of lashing out at them, but also because engaging with other human beings was just too draining. Other people's normal lives and daily struggles seemed minuscule to me (yes, I know that sounds selfish and in many ways it is but that is a part of the journey I went through). All I wanted to do was be petty about it. Again, the few and the brave who braced the icy winter of my journey probably got way more than they bargained for. By this time I was totally and completely done apologizing or explaining myself away. (In hindsight, I realise that this too is a coping mechanism. It is a method of self-preservation and it's okay to go through it, it's just not okay to stay there forever.)

Then, on a series of days, without my knowledge and / or permission, something changed. I randomly began to get the message that my voice (even through this season) needed to be heard because it gave hope to others. The two most memorable days are November 11th and November 16th. At the crack of dawn on the 11th of November as I sat at an airport terminal waiting to board a plane to a desolate destination, I bumped into a childhood friend. We had long ceased to see one another physically, but thanks to the wonders of social media, we kept abreast of one another's movements and adventures. We stopped and chatted for a bit and planned a coffee for later in the year as we parted, she said something that stopped me in my tracks and really made me think. She said (and I paraphrase) that from time to time, she would start her day by going to my social media pages for inspiration and a lot of times it stopped her from reacting to a situation in her life and allowed her to breath and think twice before doing something emotional.

The second incident came a few days later via social media. Someone I had reached out to about a month prior to that finally responded to a private message and told me that she loved my Instagram page because "I encourage her a lot". Just to be clear, I have met this person a couple of times over the past five years (in person) and our entire social interaction has been on the streets of the World Wide Web. This caught me completely off guard. I had written to her asking for her number for some professional services. Nothing personal. In her response, she added that I encourage her. These two days in the month of November stopped me right in my tracks.

They stopped me for a myriad of reasons, but more than anything, they stopped me because they reminded me that I had a responsibility to myself, to my Father in heaven and to my Daddy with wings. A responsibility to those who loved me, to those who were going through, as well as to those I may never meet but who would one day meet me through my words. That responsibility was to live my best life ever, and to be the best version of me I could possibly be. I had a responsibility beyond my grief and outside of my feelings to look beyond the here and the now to be the person I was created to be, to go through this season, come out and still live. My Daddy would not have wanted me to die with him and truth be told, no matter how hard I didn't want to be, I am still here and therefore I have a responsibility to be present and engaged. As I sit here in the wee hours of the morning listening to some Ed Sheeran and punching away on this keyboard, I am once again reminded that I have a gift - the gift of the gab. I am required to share this gift of writing with the world. These two incidences reminded me of my why. Why I am here. I am here on this earth to share this gem of greatness, this gift of writing and inspiration with you.

My message to you today

Today, I pray that my hug from the Father will also be yours. I pray that you remember your "why" and you arise and begin to live the best version of you for you, for those gone before us, for me and for the world.

Father, thank you for showing me the seed of greatness in me from a very early age. Thank you for surrounding me with an amazing support system in my family, friends, my circle and my tribe. Thank you for putting people in my life who push me to be greater than I thought I could be especially when I don't feel like putting in the work and going the extra mile. I know Lord that not everyone has fully understood their why and that some even struggle with the notion of purpose - the ideology that they were put on this earth for a reason and that there is something they must accomplish. Today Lord, I pray that you will begin to reveal their why to them and that you will bring people into their lives to validate their why to them. Help this be a turning point for them in this journey. A reason to do the things that would make their loved ones proud of whom they will become.

Psalm 57:2

I cry out to God, the Most High, to God who always does what is good for me.

Today I Struggled With

(Write down the thing you are scared to say out loud or face. This will help give you the courage to face it)

....
....
....
....
....

Today I Overcame

(Write down even the smallest of things - they are all big wins and give us the courage to move forward).

....
....
....
....
....

(Make one commitment (however big or small) that will help you begin to heal. It could be - Tomorrow I will get out of bed or answer the phone or eat a meal or cry or journal or leave the house). Write it down and be intentional about it tomorrow, however hard it may look).

....
....
....
....

26

REFLECTIONS OF MY DEEPEST FEAR

Through this journey, I have had to face many, many fears. My default setting, the way I prefer to deal with fear is to push it away by entering a space I can control. I buried myself in work. When I wasn't working, I invested in specific relationships which I found to be safe spaces free of awkward moments. I decided to be intentional with my friendships because losing someone will make you realize how much you must value those you love. The anger and the pain, if you allow them, can become so familiar that you get lost and cannot find your way back. In my case, in many instances - many relationships, I truthfully don't know if I will be able to find my way back to love. Back to happiness. Back to sunshine and rainbows. Because the valley of the shadow of death is a real place and if you don't navigate it right, you lose a lot in it. I wonder how many people walk around the streets of this life looking normal but in reality they are trudging through the valley of the shadow and barely making it from one day to the next.

For the first time in my life, I have a taste (albeit a small one) of the harsh reality that is mental health issues and even depression. I can now better understand and not just form a place of empathy, how someone can contemplate suicide - not from a selfish place, but from a desperate place. I have asked myself on more than one occasion how to wake up and pushed myself to get out of bed. I have looked around, not wanting to die, but not knowing how to live. I never contemplated self-hurt or even mutilation. It's not about what you think about doing, but about what you simply don't know how to do anymore.

Today, I will speak of my deepest fear. The past few months it has been hard to pray. I have tried to and faked it and sometimes just outright refused to. I know with my logical mind that God loves me and that He is right here carrying me through this valley. However, my logical mind is doing a very poor job of rationalizing this to my aching heart. If I'm being brutally honest, I admit that my deepest fear is not being able to find my way back to God. Being unable to pray and to communicate with Him because this huge boulder of grief sitting on my chest makes me sometimes unable to breathe. Because you see, my foundation, the reason I can look forward to a tomorrow is because I have known and been loved by the One who orders and ordains all of my tomorrows. Not being able to feel God, or being too hurt, weak or angry to speak to Him gives me chills. If I did not have my relationship with my heavenly Father then what would I have to hold on to? What would I have to hope for? The struggle inside of me that has almost torn me apart has been between knowing, on the one hand that He loves me and has my future in His hands, while conversely knowing that He allowed my Daddy to die. I know part of it is selfish because I know with my logical mind that my Daddy is no longer in pain, and yet not being able to see him smile or hear his voice or just know that he is here, that selfish part of me sometimes threatens to pull me into a forever abyss of nothingness and mistrust of my Father in heaven. There, I said it - I have trust issues with God!

My mind and my heart, my spirit and my flesh, they constantly battle inside this tired and fragile soul. They constantly and consistently buffer one another and I am so tired. They do this for so long until one day the dam bursts. I stop trying to control the situation. I stop refusing to cry and I lay in my bed and cry for three days. I stand in the shower and I weep and I talk to God - angry whispers, torturous whimpers, until I have nothing left. Not anger, not strength, not joy, not answers, not fear, and not courage. Just nothing. Then, I sleep a deep, dreamless, peaceful sleep. And here's how I began to heal, here's my little secret. The only way I found my way back to love, the love of my Father, was by letting go. I stopped trying to control things, and started allowing Him to find me in my brokenness. I finally allowed Him to take control of my anger, my tears, my fears, my hopes and my dreams. I allowed myself to be broken and He came and picked up the pieces of my broken heart and every shattered shard that had melted into a tear. He collected them all and held them as He held me as I slept.

When I emerged from those three days, I knew one thing for sure. God doesn't need my permission to love me. He doesn't need my help to find me. He doesn't need my words to hear me. He is not blind to my pain and my tears, even when He doesn't speak audibly. When I allowed Him into my broken place, He led me back to my safe space. Back to love. I'm not all the way there. I still have moments when prayer seems like a foreign concept. In all this I know that a tear, a whisper, a sigh or just saying the name of Jesus, just that, and that alone, is enough for Him. My brokenness is more than enough for Him. He doesn't need me to do anything other than just to let Him in. Now, instead of controlling it, sometimes I allow myself to sit in it with Him, and not say anything. Because sometimes, words just aren't enough and silence speaks louder than anything my mind could fathom or my mouth could form. In those times, I do all I know to do. I allow my silence and His silence to be the hug I need for that day.

My message to you today

Receive your Hug today knowing that you are more than enough and that your pain speaks to His heart. It's okay to be afraid - allow yourself to go through the fear and come out on the other side. Allow yourself to find your way back to love, to sunshine and to rainbows.

Prayer

Father, thank you for allowing me to go through the season of mistrust. Thank you for allowing me to hit rock bottom. Thank you for allowing me to break completely. But most of all, thank you for finding your way into my heart through the anger, the bitterness, the sadness, the questions, and loving me back to you. Thank you for your unconditional love. Even when I don't act right. Even when I reject it. Even when the interpretation thereof confuses me. Thank you for patiently allowing me to go through and never leaving nor forsaking me inspite of my humanity. Thank you for love. Today I pray that someone out there will allow themselves to break. That they will allow themselves to hit rock bottom. That they will let go and stop trying to explain or control their situation and that at that point, they will let you in and in so doing find their way back to love.

Romans 8:35, 38 - 39

...So who can separate us? What can come between us and the love of God's Anointed? Can troubles, hardships, persecution, hunger, poverty, danger, or even death? The answer is, absolutely nothing...

...For I have every confidence that nothing—not death, life, heavenly messengers, dark spirits, the present, the future, spiritual powers, 39 height, depth, nor any created thing—can come between us and the love of God revealed in the Anointed, Jesus our Lord...

Today I Struggled With

(Write down the thing you are scared to say out loud or face. This will help give you the courage to face it)

....
....
....
....
....

Today I Overcame

(Write down even the smallest of things - they are all big wins and give us the courage to move forward).

....
....
....
....
....

Tomorrow I Will

(Make one commitment (however big or small) that will help you begin to heal. It could be - Tomorrow I will get out of bed or answer the phone or eat a meal or cry or journal or leave the house). Write it down and be intentional about it tomorrow, however hard it may look).

....
....
....
....
....

27

REFLECTIONS OF LOSING EVERYTHING & GAINING EVERYTHING

The journey of grief and loss is a weird one. One moment you can be laughing until your ribs hurt and the next crying until you cannot breathe. The one thing I have gained along this journey is perspective. I now have the ability to say "NO" to the things that don't matter, "MAYBE" to the things that can wait, and "YES" to everything else in between. I have gained the courage to be bolder than I ever was. I have gained the courage to face my fears. I have gained the wisdom to know the difference between what really, truly matters and the people, places and things that are truly just time wasters. My Daddy was sick for a few years, and during those years, I realize now that I had stopped living for me. Every little thing that I did was centered around my Mummy and my Daddy. When a loved one is ill for a prolonged period of time that tends to happen. The beauty about this is that it allows you to say the things you wanted to say and hopefully live without regret when you do lose them. That said nothing prepares you for the moment they pass on, or the pain, heartache and shattered dreams in the days, months and years thereafter. When you finally begin to emerge from the fog, it is with a clarity of purpose. You almost lost your way when you lost them, but you learn to fight your way through the fog and the darkness hopefully emerging to live to make them proud.

For me, not holding back and living my best life means I have gained the perspective to eat life with a big spoon. It doesn't always come immediately and it may take longer for some than it does for others. It may also come seasonally when sometimes you live large and sometimes you recede in order to recharge - gain clarity and perspective based on where you are in your journey. You may even need a nudge every once in a while. For me, that nudge came one day as I was talking to my most amazing mother. I asked her how she remained so strong. We talked about that most intimate moment when we both looked down at Daddy and knew he was gone on that cold June evening. We wondered if he had heard everything we said to him in those last moments. I told her that my heart literally shattered but I felt I needed to stay strong for her. She said the single most profound thing to me - She told me that as she looked down at him and his big brown eyes were closed, she said to herself "There goes my everything." She wondered how she would survive. In that instant she raised her eyes and looked up across the bed and I was standing there holding his hand - my big, brown eyes heavy with sorrow and hopelessness. She was jolted by her next thought. She saw him in me - not just the uncanny resemblance that I bare to him physically, but the strength, courage and gentleness that he always had for her and for us. She told me that in that moment she knew that a part of him - the best part of him would remain forever with her. When she looked at me and thought of the rest of my siblings and her beautiful grandchildren, God reminded her that He had already thought about her and had a good plan for her, for us all. The next thought that jumped into her mind was "Here stands my everything."

I have slowly come to the realization that legacy is not material. Daddy's legacy will always and forever be the way I live my life. How happy I am.

The things I accomplish. The person I become. Once that dawned on me, I made up my mind there and then that I would no longer live my life for people. I would strive to do whatever it takes to live my life for me - because in the end, that's all he ever really wanted for me. In that moment, I became fully aware that although my everything was gone in him, He had given me my everything by giving me a new lease on life. I did not just lose him - I gained the true meaning of life. That, my friends, is the greatest gift my beloved Daddy could ever have given me. He was amazing in life and continues to be amazing even in death. He is in heaven looking down on me and smiling because He knows I will make him proud.

My message to you today

Today, my counsel to you is simple: do whatever it takes to make those who you have lost proud. Forgive yourself, forgive them, and strive to be happy. Grief will tell you that you need to be sad and miserable in order for it to make sense. It will lie to you that in order for your grief to be real, you should not smile or laugh or be happy in those moments and if you do then you are forgetting them or betraying their memory. I beg to differ. They would not have wanted you to live a lifetime of grief, tormented by the ghosts of yesteryears. Be happy when you can and smile when you want to. It is only in doing so that you can truly live out the legacy they would have wanted you to live. Be happy, smile and be glad that you had them for the time you did. Live your life to the fullest and eat life with a big fat spoon. After all, life is for living. That, my dear one, is your Hug from the father today.

Prayer

For anyone struggling to live, I pray today that you receive a breath of fresh air, a refreshing boost of life, laughter and energy. I pray that you learn to live again. I pray that you make the decision today and for always to shut out the feelings of survivor's guilt and that you truly gain perspective and live to make them proud. I pray that your heart confirms what your mind already knows - that you can only honour and celebrate them by living as you always should have. Living as they would have wanted you to live.

Romans 15:13

I pray that God, the source of all hope, will infuse your lives with an abundance of joy and peace in the midst of your faith so that your hope will overflow through the power of the Holy Spirit.

Today I Struggled With

(Write down the thing you are scared to say out loud or face. This will help give you the courage to face it)

....
....
....
....
....

Today I Overcame

(Write down even the smallest of things - they are all big wins and give us the courage to move forward).

....
....
....
....
....

Tomorrow I Will

(Make one commitment (however big or small) that will help you begin to heal. It could be - Tomorrow I will get out of bed or answer the phone or eat a meal or cry or journal or leave the house). Write it down and be intentional about it tomorrow, however hard it may look).

....
....
....
....
....

28

REFLECTIONS OF JINGLE BELLS AND CHRISTMAS TALES

December 31st 2018

So Christmas came and went. Ironically, the 25th of December marked exactly 6 months since Daddy's demise. I can tell that I have grown even as I have written the past 27 Chapters. There are things I would never have said 6 months ago - words I would never have used. Words like "demise". It always sounded so harsh to me. I remember in those early days people referring to my Daddy as the deceased or the late. Worse still, hearing them say things like "the remains" or "the body". It was so painful. Death has its own language. It speaks its own tongues and sings its own dirges. The people around you, however well meaning, may never understand how deeply some of the words cut you. The people around you are just navigating this journey as best as they can. (forgive me as I continue to digress every once in a while].

I have grown and for that I am grateful. No matter how much I grew, as the days went by, I began to dread Christmas Day. I mean a real fear overcame me. (Fear seems to have been a big part of my journey and I thank God for the strength to write this book as it has allowed me to first accept, then own, then confront, and finally overcome that fear!) Just the thought of it made me want to vomit. I started having mini-panic attacks. I could not bear the thought of my first Christmas without Daddy. I know for a fact that the rest of my siblings and my mother too - each of us in our little pockets or grief thought about that day and didn't know how it would go. But then God did something amazing.

Psalm 23 goes a little something like this:

The Eternal is my shepherd, He cares for me always. He provides me rest in rich, green fields beside streams of refreshing water.

He soothes my fears; He makes me whole again, steering me off worn, hard paths to roads where truth and righteousness echo His name.

Even in the unending shadows of death's darkness, I am not overcome by fear. Because You are with me in those dark moments, near with Your protection and guidance, I am comforted.

You spread out a table before me, provisions in the midst of attack from my enemies; You care for all my needs, anointing my head with soothing, fragrant oil, filling my cup again and again with Your grace.

Certainly Your faithful protection and loving provision will pursue me where I go, always, everywhere. I will always be with the Eternal, in Your house forever.

I simply cannot begin to tell you how this unfolded and became so real to us. You see some of the things I feared (in no particular order of importance) were:

a) Going home to the village to look upon the grave - now don't get me wrong, that will happen but I just wasn't ready to do it over Christmas.

b) Being in Nairobi alone/just us as a family, alone in our misery as revelry surrounds us because life goes on.

c) Being apart from my family

d) Being among people but feeling alone and lonely

On and on and on the list can go. But God! That phrase has been my sustenance and my support these past weeks. Let me explain. To me, that phrase means that regardless of what has been hurled my way, regardless of what the devil may have wanted to use to crush me, regardless of my fears or mistakes or failings, God's love for me is all I will ever need. It means that I may have been crushed, I may have been devastated, I may be imperfect, I may be nasty, I may not be able to control my emotions or words or thoughts or actions, But God. He is love and His love supersedes any and every thing that could ever try to engulf, destroy, define or refine me. But God means that regardless of me, He remains God in every situation.

Now let me come back and explain how that fits in with my Christmas tale. I am a Christmas freak. I love it all, the lights, the presents, the carols, the snow (and no, there's no snow in a typical Kenyan Christmas but in my heart, "Let it snow, let it snow, let it snow!") I love the rainy and hot December days in our warm Nairobi. I love getting together with friends, I love laughing and chilling. I love road trips. My Christmas tree literally comes up right after my birthday at the end of October and doesn't go down until the end of January. I love Christmas! Before you jump to conclusions, I don't forget the real reason for the season. I love the Christmas story and the message behind God's love for me, for us, for humanity. Again I digress. With all of the above, you can now see why I was dreading Christmas this year. I just didn't think it would hold the same memories. I didn't think it would make sense. I didn't think it would be right without Daddy - But God! He had already prepared a table for us.

For you to grasp the fullness of how God's plans began way before we even know what we need I have to begin to tell this tale decades ago. One hot January morning in 1989, my two younger sisters and I transferred to a new school. My brother already attended this school. I didn't want to go, I liked my old school. My Daddy drove us to school that morning. My brother wasn't feeling well and got sick in the car - my newly pressed grey school skirt bore the collateral damage of his breakfast. We turned back because I had to change. That meant that I was late for class that day. The first person who befriended me in spite of my negative energy and less than positive attitude that morning was a skinny little girl in pig-tails. Her name is Lola and she remains my best friend to this day. Lola had a younger sister who happened to be in the same kindergarten class as my brother. Fast forward years later and the two little munchkins (not so little any more) got married on the 18th day of December 2011. Our Daddies, who had become friends over the years became brothers and our Mummies, who had stayed up nights worrying about all of us solidified their sisterhood. The former two began planning a beautiful trip to visit each other's villages. You see most urban Kenyans don't live where they were born or raised. My Daddy was raised in Vihiga and Lola's Daddy in Kaloleni. The trip to Kaloleni should have taken place in 2012 soon after the grand wedding but Daddy's health began to fail that year and the trip never materialized. The trip to Vihiga was ill-fated because the first time my other Daddy (Lola's Daddy) visited Vihiga was to lay his brother, my Daddy to rest.

But then the most amazing thing happened. My other family (Lola's family) my brother Sidney's family planned an amazing trip in December of 2018. December of the year that we buried my Daddy. My entire family and I traversed the beautiful land of Kenya and spent our Christmas holidays at the coast. Two of my Mummy's sisters and their families joined us. Our Kaloleni adventure was grand. Grander than we expected or could ever have foreseen. They threw us a "welcome home" party like no other. There was dancing, singing, speeches, laughter and love.

In the interim, my sister J had just started a new job in a tropical paradise of a location (less than an hour from Kaloleni), and so we ended up spending our actual Christmas day in a coastal paradise. Traditionally, I'm sure, we should have spent it in Vihiga - in darkness and sadness and maybe even self-pity. But God had already prepared for us a table in paradise.

The 23rd Psalm sums it all as follows

"The Eternal is my shepherd, He cares for me always. He provides me rest in rich, green fields beside streams of refreshing water. He soothes my fears; He makes me whole again,
steering me off worn, hard paths to roads where truth and righteousness echo His name.

Even in the unending shadows of death's darkness, I am not overcome by fear. Because You are with me in those dark moments, near with Your protection and guidance, I am comforted.

You spread out a table before me, provisions in the midst of attack from my enemies; You care for all my needs, anointing my head with soothing, fragrant oil, filling my cup again and again with Your grace.

Certainly Your faithful protection and loving provision will pursue me where I go, always, everywhere. I will always be with the Eternal, in Your house forever.

My message to you today

For anyone who is dreading Christmas, the birth, death, and resurrection of Christ all those years ago ensures that no matter what, there will always be a way of escaping our darkness and walking under the anointing and covering and into the protection and provision of our heavenly Father. Merry Christmas earthlings, from my heart to yours. Receive your Hug from the Father today and know that I am praying for each and every one of you.

Prayer

Father, just as you surprised us and loved on us on the most important day of the year - the day when we celebrate the birth of your son, I ask that you will love on those out there who need it. Not only today but also during their first Christmas, and every Christmas thereafter. Surprise them with good things and let them truly celebrate and not remember the season in bitterness and aloneness. Surround them with angels (spiritual and physical) who will love on them and help them to forget their sadness.

Today I Struggled With

(Write down the thing you are scared to say out loud or face. This will help give you the courage to face it)

....
....
....
....
....

Today I Overcame

(Write down even the smallest of things - they are all big wins and give us the courage to move forward).

....
....
....
....
....

(Make one commitment (however big or small) that will help you begin to heal. It could be - Tomorrow I will get out of bed or answer the phone or eat a meal or cry or journal or leave the house). Write it down and be intentional about it tomorrow, however hard it may look).

....
....
....
....
....

29

REFLECTIONS OF ACTUAL HUGS FROM ACTUAL FATHERS

So yesterday happened and today is here. Yesterday was last year and today we are in a different calendar year. The emotions attached with crossing over are a bag of mixed highs and lows. Because new beginnings also mean goodbyes and endings. I went through the day smiling and laughing with pockets of hidden whimpers and secret tears. Every once in a while, I would stop and cry and then put on a brave face. God gave me a lot to be thankful for this past year, despite its struggles. A lot to reflect on for this coming year 2019. I decided that come what may, I was going to cross over into the New Year in church. The New Year was going to find me acknowledging God as my one and only. After some flirtations from a flirtatious fellow (yes people, I get flirtatious too and no people, I'm not disclosing anything and no people, this is not any type of announcement), and some festivities (Le Bff is still in town for a precious few hours so had to get my last dose of her in 2018), I headed to church. I literally almost ran into a couple of people who had already over-imbibed and it was only 10pm - for those out there who think they can handle their liquor and then get behind a wheel, do you ever think of the worst case scenario? Is it ever going to be worth it? A word for 2019, Just Don't! Get a cab, a ride-share, a designated driver (there are actual apps for that these days) or stay home.

I snuck into church, well not really because I generally sit right up front and cozied up to some beautiful familiar faces. The worship at my amazing church was completely off the charts last night. My pastor got onto the pulpit an hour before midnight to give us a Word and bless us into the New Year. At some point, right as we crossed over, I broke down. Being strong isn't easy, being strong in public is darn near hard. No amount of humor and wit can mask that. I cracked because I looked down at my phone and I didn't have a missed call from Daddy. I didn't have a text message from him. The finality of the kick in the rear end that was June 25th 2018 just knocked that last wind out of me,

Then it happened, as I stood there, my Pastor came over and hugged me and wished me a happy new year. There are people out there who may not agree with me and that means they do not understand. I have been privileged in my life to know good men who covered me. My biological Daddy was one. My extraordinarily awesome mentor Fela Durotoye is another. My uncle Bishop Ken Kimiywe is a third. My gentle, humble pastor Reverend Julian Kyula is the fourth. He hugged his wife and kids, then hugged me and then went back to the pulpit to finish delivering the message. I don't know if any one of you caught the symbolism right there. I'll spell it out for you. On the one night I was crying about not receiving a hug from my Daddy, my Father above sent me a physical hug from my spiritual Father to remind me that He is still seated on the throne and that He never forgets. I know many people who have been on the tail end of abusive relationships with father figures (especially those in a place of spiritual authority over their lives). I know of them and I hear their stories and I cringe. The exact opposite applies to me. These men I mentioned above have covered me, carried me, blessed me and protected me in ways that I could never, ever describe.

Rev Julian has walked with me for almost 14 years. He has pulled gifts out of me that I did not know existed. He has corrected me in love when I needed it, carried me, covered me, celebrated me and so much more. The days Daddy was in the hospital and needed him, all I would need to do was to make a call and he would be there to pray with us. The day Daddy passed away, he and his beautiful wife Amanda (my sister friend) were at the hospital within the hour and stayed with us until the wee hours of the morning. On the day I had to bury my Daddy, he got on a plane and flew 600km away to be with my family and I. I don't know of a better example of a spiritual covering - he is to me a Father. Fast forward to December 31st 2018, circa midnight and I am standing in a sea of people feeling more alone, lost and vulnerable than I have ever felt as I crossed over into a new year feeling like I was leaving my Daddy in the old year, the first person who gave me a hug and wish me a happy new year was another Father. My spiritual Father. It was more than symbolic to me. It was my Father in heaven affirming to me that he has always been my Father. In the significance of this moment, I heard Him whisper: "I am and always will provide what you need, when you need it. I already planned for it before you knew you would be here and need it. I've got you Baby Girl. I've got this." He sent me a Hug from the Father through a father. The tears came for a bit, but they were different tears. Tears acknowledging that 2019 is going to be different, and different carries with it goodness and sweetness.

My message to you today

This message is specifically for anyone out there who is missing their Daddy today and cannot be with them, here is my word to you - find a covering, find a home, hide yourself under a father figure and let him do all the spiritual heavy lifting that your path may be made easier.

Find someone who will pray over you, support you, be honest with you, guide you and lead in love and humility. Find someone who will provide the hug (spiritual, virtual or otherwise) on the days you feel completely lost. If you have one of those, reach out today and tell them just how special they are to you. That, my friends is your Hug form the Father today.

Prayer

Today I want to pray for anyone who has experienced heartache and abuse at the hand of someone who was supposed to cover, protect and guide you. I pray that you will find a place of healing and that you will let go of the hurt. I pray that you will come to a place of peace and reconciliation knowing that the other person may not always acknowledge or apologise. I pray today that you will find your place of healing and peace to be able to move forward in your own truth. Finally, I pray that God will lead you to a place where you finally find a covering that will love, protect, preserve and guide you as only a father can.

Ephesians 4:31-32

Banish bitterness, rage and anger, shouting and slander, and any and all malicious thoughts—these are poison. 32 Instead, be kind and compassionate. Graciously forgive one another just as God has forgiven you through the Anointed, our Liberating King.

Today I Struggled With

(Write down the thing you are scared to say out loud or face. This will help give you the courage to face it)

....
....
....
....
....

Today I Overcame

(Write down even the smallest of things - they are all big wins and give us the courage to move forward).

....
....
....
....
....

(Make one commitment (however big or small) that will help you begin to heal. It could be - Tomorrow I will get out of bed or answer the phone or eat a meal or cry or journal or leave the house). Write it down and be intentional about it tomorrow, however hard it may look).

....
....
....
....
....

30

REFLECTIONS OF NEW BEGINNINGS WITH NEW FRIENDS

These next two days will be written in the form of a letter to my Daddy. As a way to celebrate him.

Dear Daddy,

These past few months have brought me the most beautiful and intimate relationships. You would like the person I am becoming. Don't get me wrong: I still sometimes get moody or snap at myself or others but for the most part, I have grown. There are things I no longer indulge in simply because they are draining and time wasters. I heard of the most interesting thing the other day. A certain lady's greeting when you get through to her voicemail says: "Sorry I can't talk right now. I'm busy changing things in my life. If I don't call you back, you're one of them". I thought that was brilliant! Daddy, I have become that person. I know where to place value, I know where to spend time and I know where I simply cannot. There are people who have walked this journey far enough and others who are just beginning. Today I'll talk about the "strange bedfellows" I have made. I have met some amazing people who have walked the journey of grief and come out on the other side beautiful yet scarred. I have made friends who have been encouraged by my journey and met others who have encouraged me with theirs. With some I know beyond the shadow of a doubt that this is seasonal. With others I pray earnestly for the relationships and the intimacy to continue to grow eternally. It doesn't mean that all my friends have changed or that I want them to, it just means that I have changed and while some people have changed with me, others have come along and connected with the changed person in me. Yet a third group have allowed me to change even as they themselves changed and we are now re-acquainting ourselves with one another as new seasons.

I have come full circle with certain things - I still miss you and always will. I still dread certain days and that may never change. I still have questions that God may or may not answer. But above all, I know beyond the shadow of a doubt that you are so very happy where you are. It is well with my soul only because your soul is with the Father and that makes all the difference. You were my rock and my foundation - You still are Daddy. That will never change. Healing is still a myth, a rumor, a very foreign concept but daily you continue (and will continue to) show me how to get by. Thank you.

Today's letter is short because I have peace, peace that surpasses human understanding. Peace like a river truly enveloping my soul and bandaging my wounds. One of my new friends asked me recently to assure her that it gets better. Without blinking, I said, "It gets easier to cope. Easier to think about them and not fall apart. Easier to face the days. Easier to smile and remember them fondly." It has not gotten easier to live without you my Daddy but you have helped to make it easier to go through the days. When my cloudy days loom, I cry. When the sunny days peak through the clouds I laugh. I no longer feel guilty when I have to do either one. You, my beloved Daddy are and always will be my hero. Rest well my Daddy. See you on the other side. Keep a place for us close to you in heaven.

My message to you today

For anyone going through, I promise, it gets better, it becomes more possible to cope day by day. Rest tonight knowing that the same God who has brought me along this journey is the very same God who will bring you out on the other side. I am not 100% okay. I still have sessions with my grief counsellor. I still break down and cry and scream. I still avoid certain people, places and things. Above all, I am stronger, wiser, better - I must be because I want to make him proud of me. Receive your Hug from the Father today knowing this, if tomorrow isn't a better day, that's still okay, but a day will come when it is a better day. Remember to reach out if you just need a hug from me today. It may not be well right now, but it shall be well with you one day soon.

Prayer

Father thank you for bringing me to this place of peace. Today I will not say a long prayer. I ask only that you will bring anyone who reads these words to their place of peace in spite of their process. I love you. Thank you for loving me. Help them to know that you love them too.

Today I Struggled With

(Write down the thing you are scared to say out loud or face. This will help give you the courage to face it)

....
....
....
....
....

Today I Overcame

(Write down even the smallest of things - they are all big wins and give us the courage to move forward).

....
....
....
....
....

(Make one commitment (however big or small) that will help you begin to heal. It could be - Tomorrow I will get out of bed or answer the phone or eat a meal or cry or journal or leave the house). Write it down and be intentional about it tomorrow, however hard it may look).

....
....
....
....
....
....
....

31

REFLECTIONS OF A GOODBYE KISS: FOREVER DADDY'S LITTLE GIRL

I miss you every single moment of every single day. I don't know if I will ever get over this or how tomorrow will look like. Every time I think of giving up, your smile and your gentle voice reminds me that you believe in me and that your biggest joy was to see me happy. I continue to do the things I know would make you proud of me.

February 13th 2019

I have so much to tell you about the past seven and a half months. Where do I even begin? I'll begin where I begin and end where the grace and strength ends because while it is an immense joy to talk to you like this, it sometimes gets incredibly hard. This job has given me so much perspective about the man you were and what you did. It's given me a little bit of insight into your work ethic, the side I never saw as a little girl. I recently got back from a work trip across this beautiful country. I was physically exhausted. Some of your grandbabies "picked me up" from the airport and excitedly babbled in their loud, high pitched voices, each of them competing for my attention. That was only three out of the seven. How on earth did you do this with the six of us? I remembered how you would come home and still have time for us, or now that I am an adult, I understand that you deliberately made time for us despite how tired you were. You asked about our day(s). You asked about school. About anything and everything we were doing. As we grew into our adult years, we would often joke about Daddy and Mummy's "21-Questions" sessions the moment we walked through the door. This time there were no 21questions from you but I can assure you Guga (grandpa), that le munchkin crew has done a great job in taking over. I was asked what kind of work I did that made me sleep out of the house. I said it was big people work. I was asked what kind of big people work specifically (not that it's a word they can pronounce) - I said numbers. I was then asked what about the letters? Did I do a lot of letters as well? I said that I did. Daddy you would be so tickled by these little people that have so much of you in them. They still remember you. They still look at your picture and ask about you. They still love you. We all miss you.

What else have I learned in these past months without you? I have learned that the presence of an active father in your life is a blessing. The way I would bounce ideas off of you at any time of the day (or night) and you always picked up and you always gave me the bluntest and most candid answer. The way you observed the things I did, the people I associated with and gave me the bluntest and most candid of opinions. The way you desired to see me publish my writing and here it is (too little too late sometimes I think but at the same time I had to begin with you didn't I?), get my PhD (we're still debating about that), and achieve so much more, that was and still is a big blessing. The way you prayed for me Daddy, every morning, every evening and every time in between. All I had to do was call and ask and you would stop whatever you were doing and bless me or pray over an issue I was having. The simplicity of your prayers, childlike almost but so direct and to the point. How I would kneel and you would place your hand on my head and bless my day. Thank you for teaching me how to pray over my future children.

These last two chapters have been the hardest to write. I have battled with a lot but mostly the fact that with the end of this book comes the end of our intimate moments because I will now share you with the world. You know what? I think you are worth sharing. The love you showed me and my siblings, my darling Daddy, as much as you were a gift to me in life and are a gift to heaven in eternity, you will continue to bring the gift of healing to so many through this story. As selfish as I want to be with you, I will not hold onto you but will share you with the world. My Hug from the Father today is that I have managed to get through this without shedding a single tear. I have smiled through most of it and that in itself is miraculous. The grief and sadness still comes in waves but for today my grief journey is a celebration of who you were, are and will always be to me. Thank you for walking tall and proud and allowing me to stand on your shoulders and see the world. Thank you for refining my pallet and sharpening my mind to be bigger, better and brighter. Thank you for the gift of laughter - I often burst out laughing as I drive to work after I see something funny or silly and wonder what remark you would have had for it. Thank you for loving us fiercely, completely, unconditionally, protectively, funnily and wholesomely. Thank you for hugging me tight and letting me go when I needed to (regardless of how hard it must have been for you as a father to watch me walk away). Just as you did that, you gave me wings to fly. Now watch me soar and make you proud. I love you Daddy. Today I'm sending a special delivery to heaven - a Hug to my Father. This journey has been a tough one and I could not have done it without you. I love you now and forever.

Forever Daddy's Little Girl

My Message to you today

It took me a very long time after completing this book to write this bit. Probably because I needed time to process everything I have been through and still be able to look back with an objective eye. My tone and language have both changed as the chapters rolled by, mostly because my point of view has also changed. Time does heal. It doesn't heal the way I generically thought about healing. What it does do is give you the space to process and find coping mechanisms as long as you need them so that you learn a new way to breathe, a new way to think, a new way to feel, a new way to live.

I am writing this on the 28th of June 2019. Three days after my Daddy's 1st Heaven-Versary. It was a tough day, but a beautiful one. That's what time does. It allows you to have a tough day but still see the beauty therein. On that day, I buried a friend, mourned my father, had a conversation that led to a beautiful new beginning, and savoured the sunset. Bitter-sweet. I celebrated with happy tears. What time allowed me to do was to be conscious of the fact that he is no longer on earth but happy about the fact that he is in heaven smiling down. It allowed me to appreciate the bitter with the sweet but appreciate them altogether.

What time has done is take away the panic attacks (time, love, prayers and therapy - if I'm being honest). I no longer experience them. Time has allowed that season to pass. Time has allowed the anger stage to fade (for the most part). Time has not and will never bring my Daddy back. But what it does and has done is allow me to fully appreciate who he was. The hole is still there. I shudder at the thought of walking down the aisle on my wedding day without him. I am deeply saddened by the truth that my children will never know him. But through the memories and love he left me, I am confident that he will forever be a part of me and hence a part of my infinite tomorrows.

To you out there reading this, wherever you are, whatever you're experiencing, know this, It does get better. Your truth and your reality are forever altered but it will get better. I promise.

Know this, I poured myself into this book just for you. This is my last hug to you from our Father in heaven. You are loved. You are treasured. You are not alone and it will get better.

Remember now and remember always that all you will ever need to get you through the tough moment or day or week of month is a Hug From The Father.

Never forget to remember that God's love for you is unconditional. It will never cease and it will never end. God loves you intensely even when you don't understand His love or agree with His methods. In your process, in your season, as you grieve try to remember that.

Lastly, remember this, you were created to shine as all stars do. This season may make you feel like you have no desire or reason to live or shine but shine you must once this is past. Just as I poured my tears into this book to help you through your season, so must you pour your story into someone else to give them hope. Sing that song, write that book. Take that trip. Apply for that job. Be happy. Live because it is only in doing so that you will be able to truly shine your light on another person's dark season to give them hope and help them find the way home.

Ecclesiastes 3:11
11 and I know God has made everything beautiful for its time. God has also placed in our minds a sense of eternity; we look back on the past and ponder over the future, yet we cannot understand the doings of God.

Today I Struggled With

(Write down the thing you are scared to say out loud or face. This will help give you the courage to face it)

....
....
....
....
....

Today I Overcame

(Write down even the smallest of things - they are all big wins and give us the courage to move forward).

....
....
....
....
....

(Make one commitment (however big or small) that will help you begin to heal. It could be - Tomorrow I will get out of bed or answer the phone or eat a meal or cry or journal or leave the house). Write it down and be intentional about it tomorrow, however hard it may look).

....
....
....
....
....

32

REFLECTIONS OF ME : I AM LOVED. I AM ENOUGH.

I cannot believe that I've come to the end of this book. It is by no means the end of this journey. In some ways, every day feels like a new chapter on this journey. 3+ years of blood, sweat and tears.

Three years of me sometimes waking up to the voice of doubt snuggled under the covers of my subconscious mind, sometimes jumping up and down on my consciousness … feeding me with self doubt that I had to overcome. Three years where I had to make the conscious decision to stop doubting myself, silence the voice of fear - the fear mostly of failure - and trust my heart. Trust that my story had an audience and that audience wore the cloak of hopelessness in the face of tragedy and loss.

Three years of me comparing myself to others and even sometimes shaming myself : XXX has just released a book and so soon after such and such event. What's taken you so long? Along life's journey, you will be tempted to look at someone else and envy their progress or question your seeming lack thereof. Over the course of these three years I have learned to take my eyes off of other people's races and run my own.

Three years of sometimes hearing how strong I am when all I wanted to do was to fold into a ball of tears and not be the strong one or the mature one. Where some days it was ok to just be sad and then get up tomorrow after going through that sadness and look for the next mountain to conquer, the next giant to slay.

Three years of all that and so much more.

Over the course of the three years, I've come to the realization and acceptance of a few things:

1. I am not XXX. - and that is okay.
2. My journey is uniquely mine - and that is okay.
3. We are not in a race - and that is okay.
4. My story will speak to who it will speak to and not reach who it was never meant to reach. My audience is uniquely predestined and nobody and nothing can change that. - and that is okay
5. I needed the three years as they have been a part of my healing journey. And that is okay.
6. Three years from now, I may have yet some more to add to this journey - and that, too will be okay.

As you evolve and grow through life - through times, seasons, experiences, traumas, relationships, losses and wins, there will be incidents where you are tempted to look around and stop. When that happens (and I promise you it will), I want you to hear me crying in a loud, desperate plea … DON'T GIVE UP … YOU CAN DO IT! There may still be one chapter left in you. Let me give you a literal example. You see, this final chapter of Hugs From The Father was always meant to exist. But if you look at the chronology of the day I started in Chapter / Day 1 and the date stamp at the head of this bonus chapter, you will realize exactly how much time has passed. As you read through the pages of this book you may even recognize how my tone has changed.

I woke up a couple of months ago and two things occurred:
1. I decided to change the design of the book cover - I looked at it one day and decided that the picture on that design no longer represented who and where I am in my healing journey. The old picture (and you'll see it here in this chapter) is representative of someone who was still in the early stages of grief. I was facing my 2nd Christmas without Daddy and still finding it hard to navigate through so many aspects of life without him. While I certainly wasn't where I had been 12 months prior, I was generally sad all the time. The shadow from the valley of death hung around me everywhere I went. That picture represented sadness. The cover you see today is me telling you - I went through and I came out on the other side. I braved the elements and I'm here to tell you that there is hope in the midst of the longest winter. That the sun will shine again. You will never be the same again but you must fight to find a way to make your person proud of who you are and how you're living your life.
2. I decided to add a chapter to bundle up this gift to you as neatly as you can tie a ribbon on death and pray that your voice gives hope to others. And here you are. So remember, there just might be one more chapter left in you. Don't Give Up.

The realization came to me as a specific data point in a sequence of seemingly random events.

First, I attended Speak For Gold : a Master Class run by my mentor Fela Durotoye (FD). It helped me better understand my gift to the world and become bolder with presenting it to the world. Prior to that, I had been overly cautious and somewhat shy about putting out this first book and shouting about my gift. I learned that your unique gift, the thing that only you have that only you can give, is not just for you. It is for the world. And it's ok to present it to the world and let the world partake of it and celebrate you.

Next, I stumbled across the Happenista Project - a weekly writing and accountability space on Clubhouse run by a childhood friend, Cat Hallam. There I learned that writing is not just for when you are in the right mood, It's also a discipline. You can program / discipline your mind to enter into the correct frame of mind to be creative. I also learned the power of collaboration and the power of accountability. I literally sat down during my second week of joining this space and completed this chapter. I held myself accountable and this group of ladies cheered me on.

Finally, I attended the Science of Astounding Results (SOAR) - a Masterclass run by my friend Bankole Williams where I learned how to decode and drop negative thoughts, words, actions, emotions, energy and habits and replace them with positive ones in order to achieve my highest results and operate at that level. I'm still working on decoding and reprogramming my mind but I am acutely aware that I can do better, more often, at a higher level. It doesn't negate the sad times. It's perfectly ok to lean into those and let the experiences lead you to recognizing your loss. I'm here to tell you that it's not healthy to stay there. Not perpetually or eternally. It may feel comfortable but it's not a healthy way to live. There is something you are yet to achieve or you wouldn't be alive. Together let's go down this path of discovery. Let's see what there is to see, discover what there is to discover and live the life we are predestined to live. There is a seed of greatness inside of you . Don't you ever forget it.

I'm going to leave you with the following quote by actress Emma Stone: "What sets you apart can sometimes feel like a burden, and it's not. And a lot of the time, it's what makes you great".

If your journey is what has set you apart thus far, lean into the lessons learned and the experiences had and you will most assuredly discover greatness down the path of being set apart.

Finally, let me tell you how proud I am of you for getting to this point in the book and in your healing journey.

Remember now and remember always that
You are LOVED
You are E.N.O.U.G.H.

BIO

Born and raised in Kenya, Beverly has an Undergraduate Degree (International Relations & Diplomacy) and an MBA (International Business, Global Technology Management).

She has over 15 years of experience in Human Resource Management and currently consults in the same field for one of the world's largest humanitarian agencies.

While her title is HR, her passion is people. She loves to help people identify their purpose and equip them with the tools to achieve it.

She is a seasoned speaker, moderator, podcaster and soon to be published author, using her voice through her brand BeverlySpeaks to Equip, Empower and Enlighten.

Having worked, travelled and lived across 3 continents, Beverly currently lives in Italy where she enjoys the culture, food, people and travelling.

Beverly is passionate about God, family and her pursuit of purpose.

Beverly can be reached via email at
hugsfromthefatherbook@gmail.com or

Via her website
hugsfromthefatherbook.crd.co